Workbook

to accompany

Music
In Theory and Practice

Volume I

Seventh Edition

Bruce Benward
University of Wisconsin–Madison

Marilyn Saker
Eastern Michigan University

Prepared by
Marilyn Saker

Boston   Burr Ridge, IL   Dubuque, IA   Madison, WI   New York   San Francisco   St. Louis
Bangkok   Bogotá   Caracas   Kuala Lumpur   Lisbon   London   Madrid   Mexico City
Milan   Montreal   New Delhi   Santiago   Seoul   Singapore   Sydney   Taipei   Toronto

McGraw-Hill Higher Education

A Division of The **McGraw-Hill** Companies

Workbook to accompany
MUSIC IN THEORY AND PRACTICE, VOLUME I
Bruce Benward, Marilyn Saker

Published by McGraw-Hill, an imprint of The McGraw-Hill Companies, Inc., 1221 Avenue of the Americas, New York, NY 10020. Copyright © 2003, 1998 by The McGraw-Hill Companies, Inc. All rights reserved.

7 8 9 0 QPD/QPD 0 9 8 7 6

ISBN 978-0-07-245743-8
MHID 0-07-245743-0

www.mhhe.com

Contents

Preface

The workbook/anthologies to accompany *Music in Theory and Practice*, volumes 1 and 2, provide assignments to augment those printed in the texts and additional music for study. The chapters of the workbooks bear the same titles as those of the texts and are directly correlated with them. The pieces in the anthology sections are referred to in the assignments, but the instructor is free to use these pieces in any way he or she feels is appropriate.

The workbooks contain three different types of assignments:

1. *Drill.* This type of assignment acquaints students with the material in the corresponding chapters of the text. Learning to spell chords in various keys, distinguishing between chords in isolation, and identifying musical designs in artificially prepared situations are examples of drill exercises.
2. *Analysis.* This type of assignment acquaints students with music literature, permits them to view chapter material in its actual setting, and allows them to observe conformity to as well as digression from the norm. These exercises will also improve sight-reading ability and dexterity in analysis.
3. *Composition.* After the extensive drill and comprehensive analysis assignments, students are encouraged to try employing musical ideas, chord progressions, phrase relationships, and so on in their own musical compositions. If the devices that were drilled and analyzed can be successfully manipulated in a composition, one of the most important goals in the study of music theory will have been achieved.

The workbook/anthologies include guided review and self-testing sections. Each chapter contains a suggested strategy for reviewing and learning the material. Students often find that the study skills they have developed for other courses don't work well in learning music theory. The guided review sections present a step-by-step process involving reading, playing musical examples, and writing, which will help ensure success in learning the material.

Each chapter concludes with a sample chapter test covering the essential concepts of the chapter. Answers for all chapter tests are contained in a section beginning on page 161. These tests allow the student to identify areas of strength and weakness before in-class examinations.

The workbook for this edition of *Music in Theory and Practice* includes a CD-ROM containing the *Finale Workbook*™ tool. This new software tool, produced in conjunction with Coda Music Technology, is based on *Finale*™ notation software and is compatible with both Windows and Macintosh computers. The *Finale Workbook*™ tool permits students to complete assignments while introducing them to the use of current music-notation technology. Assignments can be printed, emailed, or posted to the web. Self-contained and easy to use, the *Finale Workbook*™ tool is a valuable addition to the seventh edition.

Also new to this edition is the support of a web site. Online resources include assignment templates for the *Finale Workbook*™ tool, music-fundamental review exercises, and additional recordings. The website can be found at www.mhhe.com/mtp7.

Bruce Benward
Marilyn Saker

1 **Notation**

A. Rewrite this melody using the clef provided. Also add proper meter and key signatures.

Saint-Saëns: Septet in E-flat Major, op. 65.

1.

2.

3.

4.

B. Write the letter name for each tone and indicate the octave identification.

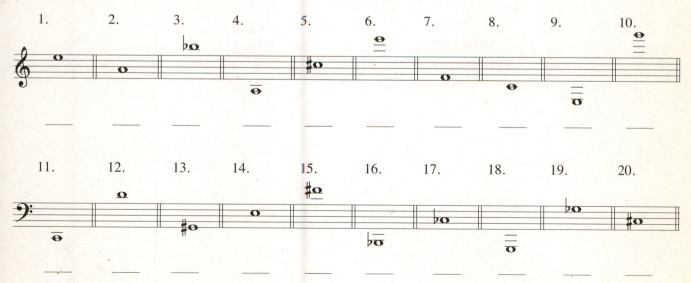

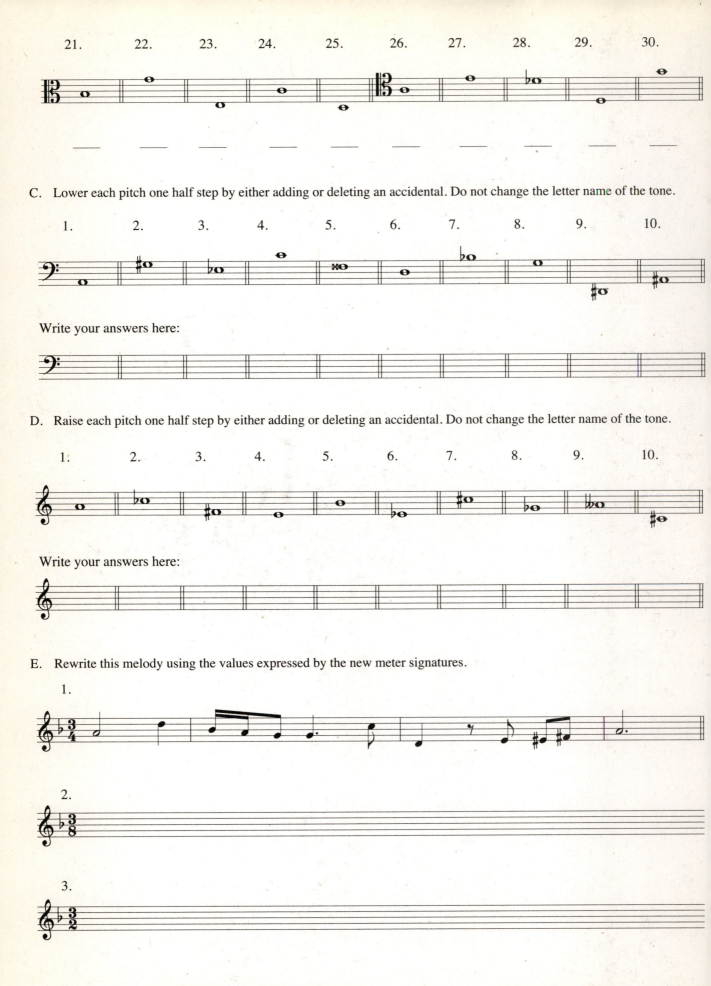

C. Lower each pitch one half step by either adding or deleting an accidental. Do not change the letter name of the tone.

Write your answers here:

D. Raise each pitch one half step by either adding or deleting an accidental. Do not change the letter name of the tone.

Write your answers here:

E. Rewrite this melody using the values expressed by the new meter signatures.

1.

2.

3.

Rewrite each phrase, correcting the errors in notation.

9.

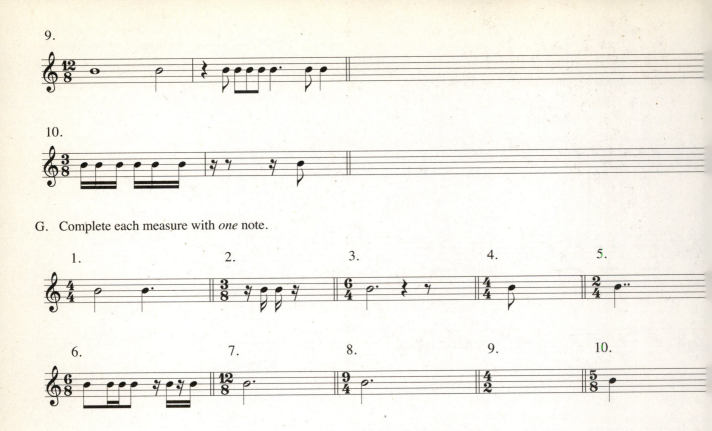

10.

G. Complete each measure with *one* note.

1.   2.   3.   4.   5.

6.   7.   8.   9.   10.

H. Write the correct meter signature for each of these measures. (In some instances, there is more than one correct answer.)

1.   2.   3.   4.

5.   6.   7.   8.   9.

I. Rewrite and correct the notation. Do not remove or change the pitch of any note.

1. Instrumental

2. Instrumental

The Fundamentals of Music

3. For piano

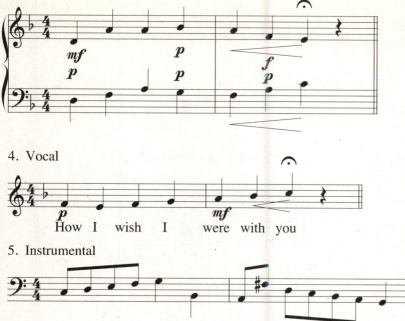

4. Vocal

How I wish I were with you

5. Instrumental

J.   On a separate sheet of paper, rewrite the following excerpt, raising each tone one half step through the use of accidentals.

K.   On a separate sheet of paper, rewrite the following excerpt, lowering each tone one half step by using the proper accidentals.

L.   On a separate sheet of paper, rewrite the following excerpt, changing the meter signature to $\frac{4}{8}$. Make sure the $\frac{4}{8}$ measures contain the same number of notes as the $\frac{4}{4}$ measures.

Schumann: *Trällerliedchen* (Humming Song) from Album for the Young, op. 68, no. 3, m. 1–4.

Nicht schnell

Review

You will find sections labeled "Review" near the end of each chapter in this Workbook/Anthology. The purpose of these sections is to provide a list of specific activities to improve your understanding of and fluency with the materials of the chapter. Music theory study is different from other academic classes you have had, and the study skills you have acquired there may not work in this class. Reading the chapter again or studying the areas you highlighted on first reading will not suffice. These materials must be practiced on a regular basis until they become second nature to you. If you take time to work on the following suggestions, you will find your knowledge and skills improving, and you will be on your way to success.

1.   Look at the list of topics at the head of the chapter (page 3 in the textbook). Try to recall as specifically as possible the content of each of the sections. If any topics seem unclear to you, target those sections for careful study.
2.   Sit at a piano keyboard. Play random white keys. For each key played, name the note, the solfeggio syllable, and the specific octave identification.
3.   Take a piece of music. Look at each note and name the half step above and below that note.
4.   Look in the anthology section beginning on page 175. Examine the meter signature of each piece and identify it as simple meter or compound meter. Can you locate a division of the beat? A subdivision? Are there any irregular divisions?

5. Take a piece of music. Copy it on a blank piece of paper. In the days before copy machines, musicians regularly copied music, and it is said that many great composers learned their craft by copying other composers' music. You must learn to produce clear, legible manuscript, and copying music and comparing your work with the original is good practice. Even though we now have computer programs to create music manuscript, you can still learn a lot about music notation by copying music by hand.

Test Yourself 1

Answers are on page 161.

1. Write the letter name of each of the following notes and indicate the octave identification.

2. Find the pairs of enharmonic equivalents among the following ten notes.

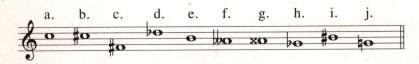

3. Find the errors in notation in each measure below.

4. Name the note one half step above each of the following notes.

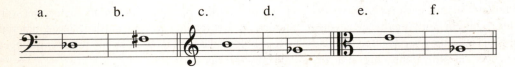

A. Add the sharps or flats (on the staff, to individual notes) needed to form each scale.

1. G♯ natural minor

2. E♭ major

3. B♭ ascending melodic minor

4. G♭ major

5. G harmonic minor

6. F ascending melodic minor

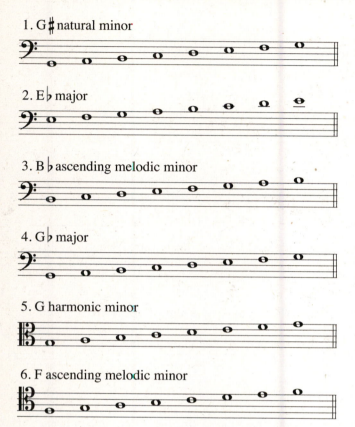

B. Each tone below is described as a degree in a particular *major* scale. Name the major key.

1.

Mediant in _____

Dominant in _____

Supertonic in _____

2.

Tonic in _____

Leading tone in _____

Submediant in _____

3.

Supertonic in _____

Mediant in _____

Submediant in _____

4.

Subdominant in _____

Dominant in _____

Supertonic in _____

5.

Mediant in _____

Tonic in _____

Subdominant in _____

6.

Leading tone in _____

Submediant in _____

Mediant in _____

C. Each tone below is described as a degree in a particular *natural* or *harmonic minor* scale. Name the minor key.

1.

Dominant in _____

Mediant in _____

Supertonic in _____

2.

Tonic in _____

Subdominant in _____

Dominant in _____

3.

Dominant in _____

Tonic in _____

Mediant in _____

4.

Mediant in _____

Subdominant in _____

Subtonic in _____

5.

Supertonic in _____

Leading tone in _____

Subdominant in _____

6.

Tonic in _____

Mediant in _____

Dominant in _____

D. Write the key signature for each of the following:

1. fm   2. AM   3. c♯m   4. D♭M   5. g♯m   6. F♯M   7. bm   8. dm   9. A♭M   10. e♭m

E. Match the column on the right with that on the left by placing the number representing the correct answer in each blank.

1. Parallel minor of F♯ major
2. Relative minor of F♯ major
3. Enharmonic with A♭ minor
4. Relative major of G minor
5. Parallel minor of A♭ major
6. Enharmonic with F♯ major
7. Relative major of C♯ minor
8. Parallel major of G minor
9. Parallel major of C minor
10. Relative minor of E♭ major

C major _____

B♭ major _____

F♯ minor _____

D♯ minor _____

C minor _____

E major _____

G major _____

G♯ minor _____

G♭ major _____

A♭ minor _____

F. Each of the following melodies is based on one of the scales listed here. Write the name of the proper scale in the blank above each melody.

Scales: Chromatic   Major   Harmonic minor   Pentatonic
         Natural minor   Melodic minor   Whole tone

G. Rewrite the following, adding or subtracting accidentals to conform to the key or mode requested.

Brahms: Symphony No. 1 in C Minor, op. 68, IV (Allegro), m. 62–65.

1. Natural minor

2. Melodic minor (ascending or descending form where appropriate)

3. Dorian mode

4. Harmonic minor

5. Mixolydian mode

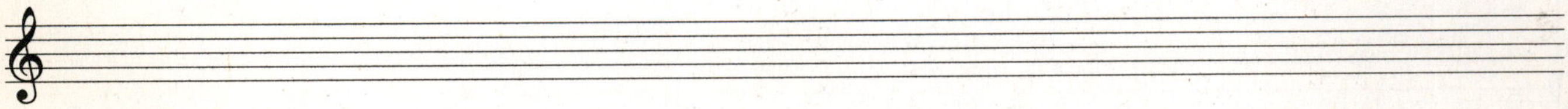

H. Add or substract accidentals to change these melodies to the mode requested.

1. Dorian mode

2. Lydian mode

3. Mixolydian mode

4. Phrygian mode

5. Aeolian mode

I. In each of the six melodies that follow:
1. Write the pitch inventory, always beginning with A.
2. Examine the melody for clues to a possible tonic note, especially observing:
    a. Direction of the melody pointing to a tonic
    b. Strong intervallic relationships stressing a central tone
    c. Cadence emphasizing a central tone
3. Go back and examine the pitch inventory to see if it can be arranged into a scale according to your findings for instruction 2.
4. Arrange the pitch inventory into a scale with the tonic as the first pitch.
5. Examine your scale to see if it fits a pattern of a mode (for example, Dorian, Phrygian), a key (major or minor), or one of the other scales introduced in chapter 2.
6. Enter this information as requested.

1.

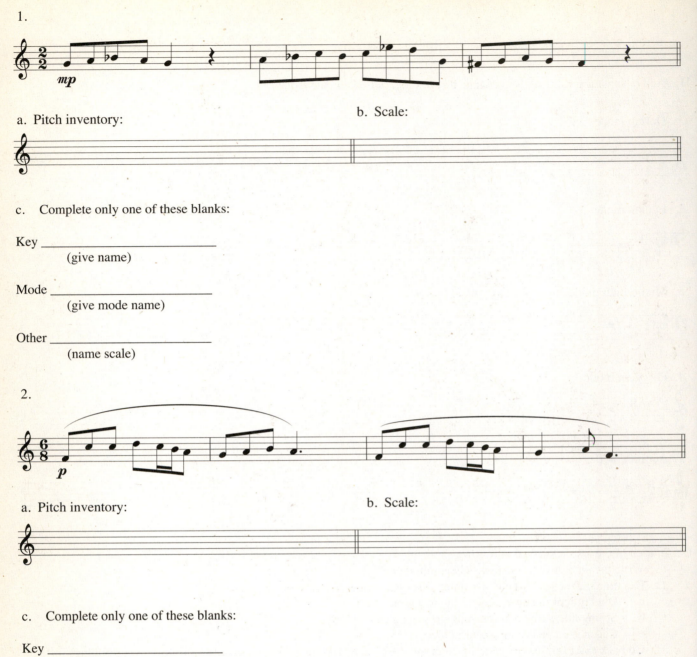

a. Pitch inventory:

b. Scale:

c. Complete only one of these blanks:

Key _____
      (give name)

Mode _____
      (give mode name)

Other _____
      (name scale)

2.

a. Pitch inventory:

b. Scale:

c. Complete only one of these blanks:

Key _____
      (give name)

Mode _____
      (give mode name)

Other _____
      (name scale)

Name ______________________________

Section ______________________________

Date ______________________________

3.

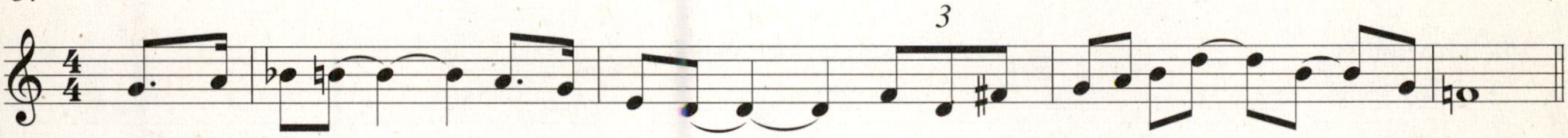

a. Pitch inventory: b. Scale:

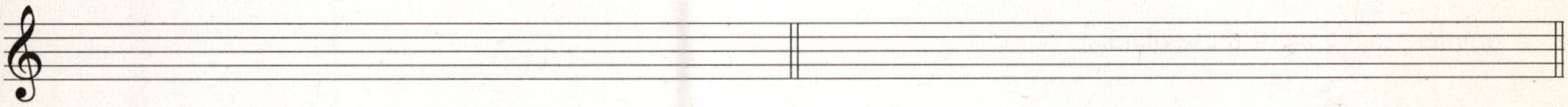

c. Complete only one of these blanks:

Key ______________________________
(give name)

Mode ______________________________
(give mode name)

Other ______________________________
(name scale)

4.

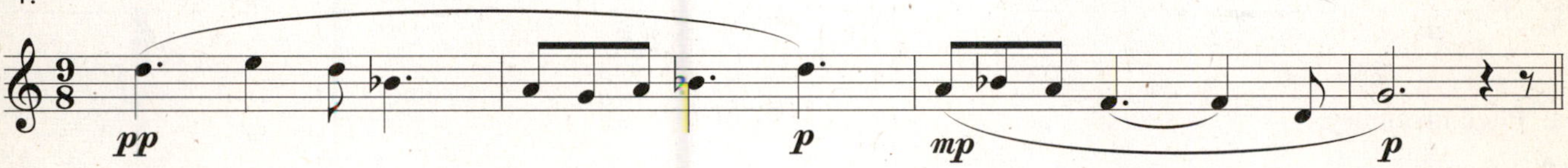

a. Pitch inventory: b. Scale:

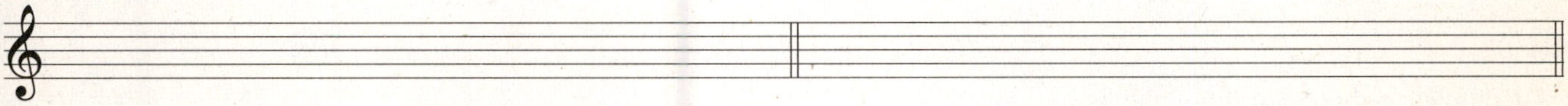

c. Complete only one of these blanks:

Key ______________________________
(give name)

Mode ______________________________
(give mode name)

Other ______________________________
(name scale)

5.

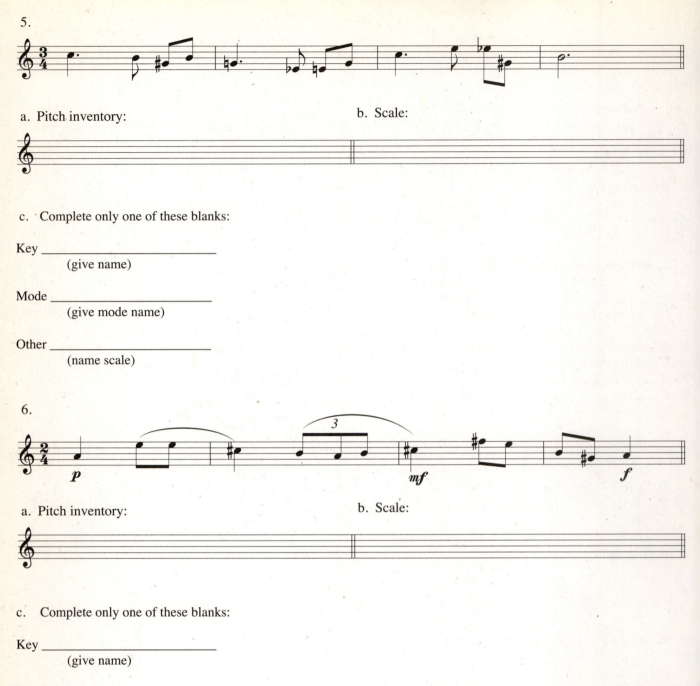

a. Pitch inventory:

b. Scale:

c. Complete only one of these blanks:

Key _____
　　　　(give name)

Mode _____
　　　　(give mode name)

Other _____
　　　　(name scale)

6.

a. Pitch inventory:

b. Scale:

c. Complete only one of these blanks:

Key _____
　　　　(give name)

Mode _____
　　　　(give mode name)

Other _____
　　　　(name scale)

J.　Refer to Rumanian Folk Song and Bagatelle, op. 6, no. 5, by Béla Bartók (1881–1945) on page 184.
　　1.　Play or sing the melody only and determine the type of scale or mode used.
　　2.　Examine the accompaniment and circle all pitches that do not conform to the scale or mode of the composition.

Review

1. Starting on C, write the key signature for the major scale on each half step. Check your work by referring to figure 2.6 in the text (page 28). Now do the same for minor scales. Check your work using figure 2.18 on page 35.
2. At the piano keyboard, play the major scale and the three forms of the minor scales beginning on each pitch. Name the notes using letter names as you play each scale.
3. Take a single note. Make it the tonic, the supertonic, the mediant, the subdominant, the dominant, the submediant, and the leading tone of a major scale. Now make it the subtonic of a minor scale. Choose another note and repeat the exercise.
4. Name the major and minor scale for each of the key signatures from seven sharps through seven flats.
5 . For each composition in the anthology look at the key signature and name the major and minor scale for that key signature. (Can you tell if the piece is in a major or a minor key?)
6. Work with a friend in spelling the major scales and the three forms of the minor scales. Take turns asking for a scale and check each other's work. See who can spell the most scales without making an error.
7. Look at the list of topics at the beginning of the chapter and review any areas for which you can't remember specific details.
8. Using familiar melodies or melodies from your sight-singing book, do a pitch inventory of several melodies. Can you identify the scale from your inventory and by examining the melody?
9. If you have computer software available for the major and minor scales, use it to review.

Test Yourself 2

Answers are on page 162.

1. Identify each of the following scales (major, natural minor, harmonic minor, melodic minor).

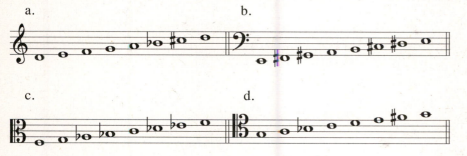

2. Name the major and the minor scale for each of the following key signatures.

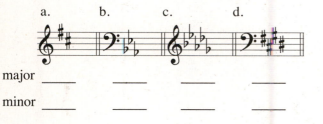

major _____   _____   _____   _____

minor _____   _____   _____   _____

3. Each of the following groups of notes is part of two major scales. Name the two scales.

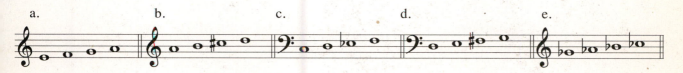

4. Add the sharps or flats (on the staff, to individual notes) to form the scale requested.

a. D major

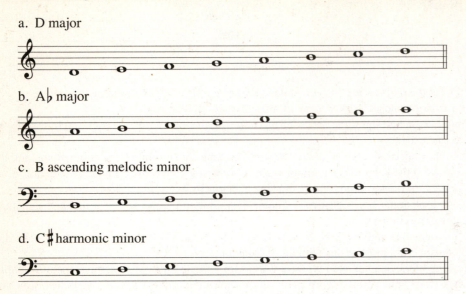

b. A♭ major

c. B ascending melodic minor

d. C♯ harmonic minor

5. Add the correct accidentals to form the mode requested.

a. Phrygian mode

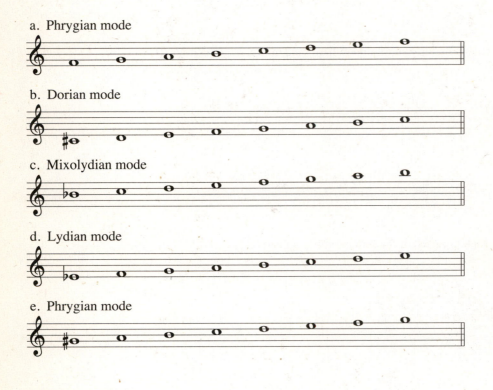

b. Dorian mode

c. Mixolydian mode

d. Lydian mode

e. Phrygian mode

A. Write the requested interval both *above* and *below* the given tone.

1. (Ex.) 2. 3. 4. 5. 6. 7. 8. 9. 10.

P5   P4   M3   m3   P4   P5   M3   m6   m3   P4

11. 12. 13. 14. 15. 16. 17. 18. 19. 20.

M6   M2   m7   m6   M2   M7   M7   m6   M6   m7

21. 22. 23. 24. 25. 26. 27. 28. 29. 30.

P5   P4   M3   m3   M3   P4   P5   P4   M3   m3

31. 32. 33. 34. 35. 36. 37. 38. 39. 40.

m7   M7   m6   M2   m2   m7   M7   m2   m7   m6

41. 42. 43. 44. 45. 46. 47. 48. 49. 50.

A5   d5   A2   d5   A4   A2   A4   d4   A4   A2

51. 52. 53. 54. 55. 56. 57. 58. 59. 60.

d7   M7   m7   M6   m6   d7   m6   M6   d7   M6

B. Here are some additional intervals to write. Write the requested interval *above* the given note. Below the given note write and label the inversion.

C. Below is a series of thirty compound intervals (intervals exceeding an octave in size).
    1. First, reduce each compound interval to its simple equivalent by transposing the upper note down an octave (or two octaves when needed) to make the interval less than an octave in size.
    2. When the compound interval has been reduced to a simple interval write its name (P5, M6, A4, etc.) in the blank provided. (Numbers 21–30 are more difficult than the first 20.)

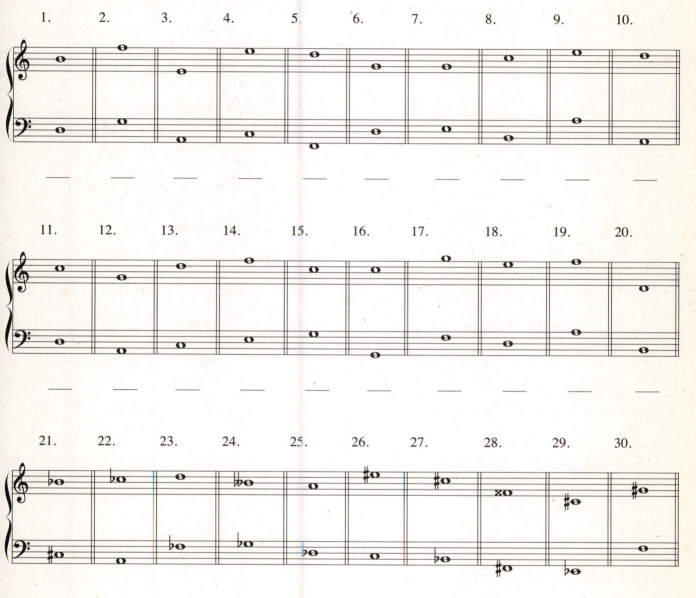

D. 1. Write the harmonic intervals between the tones of this two-voice composition. Blanks are provided between the staves.
    2. When the interval size exceeds an octave, simply subtract the octave (example: a 10th becomes a 3rd when the octave is subtracted). Intervals that exceed an octave are called *compound intervals*.
    3. Write the inversion of each interval below the staff in the blanks provided.
    4. When this is completed, rewrite the excerpt on a separate sheet of score paper, transposing the upper part down one octave and the lower part up one octave.
    5. Now write the intervals between the parts in your transposed version.
    6. Check these intervals with the inversions you wrote in no. 3 above.

Bach: Canon from the Musical Offering, BWV 1079, m. 1–6.

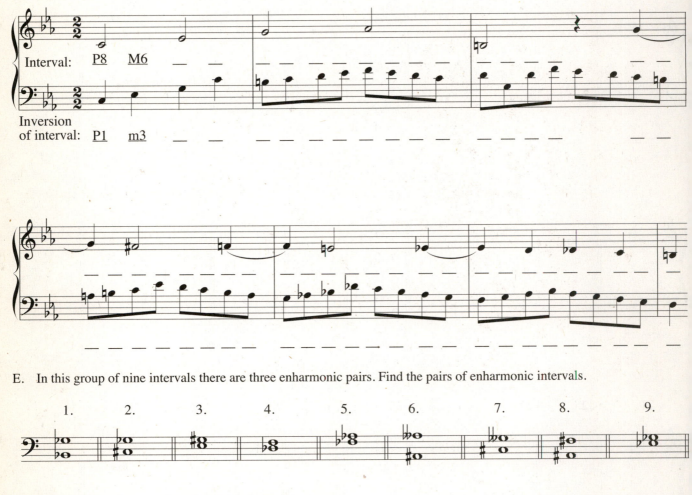

E. In this group of nine intervals there are three enharmonic pairs. Find the pairs of enharmonic intervals.

Numbers _____ and _____ are enharmonic intervals.
Numbers _____ and _____ are enharmonic intervals.
Numbers _____ and _____ are enharmonic intervals.

F. Here is a melody by Strauss. Indicate the melodic intervals (the intervals between the tones of the melody).

R. Strauss: *Don Juan,* op. 20.

From Edition Peters. Used by permission.

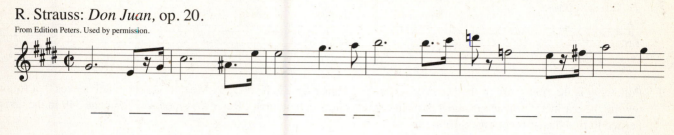

___ ___ ___ ___ ___ ___ ___   ___ ___ ___ ___ ___ ___ ___

G. Refer to *Rigaudon* from *Pièces de Clavecin* by François Couperin (1668–1733) on page 201.
 1. In the blanks below each double staff, indicate the interval between the lowest- and highest-sounding voices.
 2. All the intervals are compound (greater than an octave), so it will be necessary to subtract the octave or octaves to reduce them to simple (less than an octave) intervals.
 3. The first five intervals are provided to illustrate the procedure.

H. Rewrite the following melody for each of the instruments named below.
 1. The melody is written at concert pitch (actual pitch).
 2. Each instrument is to play the same pitches indicated in the melody. Thus, transposition is necessary in all cases except for no. 6.
 3. Be sure to include the proper key signatures.

 The melody:

 1. B-flat clarinet

 2. Clarinet in A

 3. English horn

 4. Horn in F

 5. Trumpet in D

6. Viola (To place the melody into a better range for the viola, write the notes an octave lower than printed.)

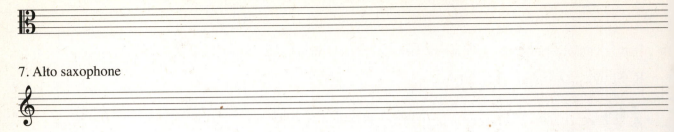

7. Alto saxophone

I. Following is the first score of the Menuetto from Symphony no. 39, K. 543, by Mozart. On the blank staves that follow, rewrite the clarinet, horn, and trumpet parts in concert pitch (actual pitch). Refer to Appendix E on page 349 in the text as needed to find the correct transposition.

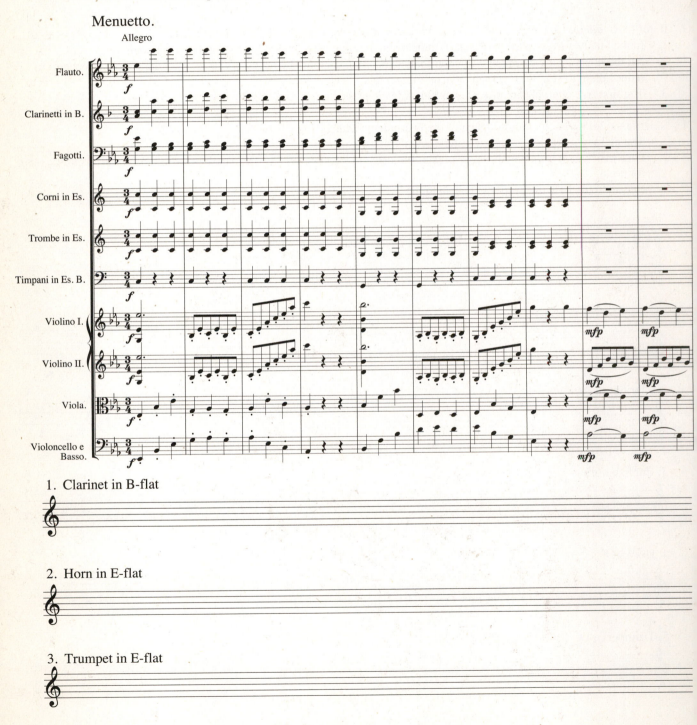

1. Clarinet in B-flat

2. Horn in E-flat

3. Trumpet in E-flat

J. Below is the introduction to Symphony no. 38, the "Prague Symphony," K. 504, by Mozart. On the blank staves below, rewrite the horn, trumpet, and string bass parts in concert pitch.

1. Horns in D

2. Trumpets in D

3. String Bass

K. Rewrite the following melody for each of the instruments named below.
    1. The melody is a B-flat clarinet part as the clarinetist would play it from a score. Thus, it is not written at concert pitch.
    2. Be sure to transpose the melody so each instrument will play the same pitches as those played by the clarinetist.
    3. Include the proper key signature for each instrument.

B-flat Clarinet

1. Oboe

2. Trumpet in B-flat

3. Horn in F

4. Alto saxophone

L. Following is the instrumentation of *Rapsodie Espagnole* by Maurice Ravel (1875–1937).
    1. The pitch given here for each instrument in the score is the written pitch.
    2. Write the concert pitch of each instrument beside the written pitch, referring to Appendix E as needed.
    3. The correct procedure is illustrated for the petite flûte.

(Ex.) Petite Flûte Grande Flûte Hautbois   Cor Anglais   Clarinette Basse Basson

Cor   Trombone   Tuba   Alto   Contrebasse

M. Following is the first page of the score of *Don Juan*, op. 20, by Richard Strauss (1864–1949), composed in 1888. On a separate sheet of paper write the concert pitch of each instrument playing on the first beat of measure 4 except for the timpani (pauken).

R. Strauss: Don Juan, op. 20, m. 1–5.

From Edition Peters. Used by permission.

Review

1. Look at the list of concepts at the beginning of the chapter in the text. Define each term in your own words and check your definition with the book.
2. Take one note and name each of the following intervals above that note: m2, M2, A2, m3, M3, P4, A4, d5, P5, A5, m6, M6, A6, m7, M7. Now name the same list of intervals below that note. Now select a new note and repeat the exercise.
3. Sit at a piano keyboard and play two tones at random. Name the interval. Spell one of the tones enharmonically and rename the interval. Move the lower tone up an octave, now name the interval.
4. Select a major scale. Identify all pairs of scale degrees that are a M2 apart, spelling each. Repeat this process for each interval type (refer to item 2 above). This exercise should also be practiced using a minor scale.
5. Select a major scale, name the interval between each scale degree and the remaining scale degrees. In the same way, name the intervals in the three forms of the minor scale.
6. Look at a piece of music. Name the interval between each note in the melody.
7. Work with a friend on spelling intervals.
8. Use computer software if it is available.

Test Yourself 3

Answers are on page 163.

1. Name the seven consonant intervals.

2. Identify each of the following intervals.

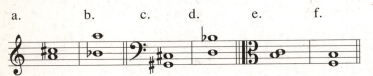

3. Name the inversion of each of the intervals in question 2.

4. Identify the intervals between the two voices below.

a. _____ b. _____ c. _____ d. _____ e. _____ f. _____ g. _____ h. _____
i. _____ j. _____ k. _____ l. _____ m. _____ n. _____ o. _____ p. _____

5. Name the note that is the requested interval *above* each of the following notes:

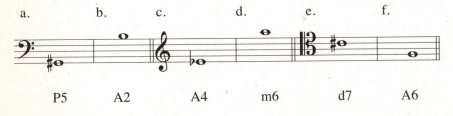

6. Name the note that is the requested interval *below* each of the notes in question 5.

4 Chords

Name _____

Section _____

Date _____

A. Indicate in the blanks below the type of triad shown. Use the following symbols:

M = Major
m = Minor
A = Augmented
d = Diminished

1.　2.　3.　4.　5.　6.　7.　8.　9.　10.

_____　_____　_____　_____　_____　_____　_____　_____　_____　_____

11.　12.　13.　14.　15.　16.　17.　18.　19.　20.

_____　_____　_____　_____　_____　_____　_____　_____　_____　_____

B. Refer to the Schumann chorale *Freu dich sehr, o meine Seele* from Album for the Young, op. 68, no. 4, on page 239. Indicate:

1. The letter name of each triad or seventh chord.
2. The type of chord:

Major = Capital letter
Minor = Small letter
Augmented = Capital letter plus +
Diminished = Small letter plus °
Major-minor seventh chord = Capital letter plus [7]

C. Refer to Handel's Hallelujah chorus on page 207. Name all the chords in each of the measures indicated below. Use the same symbols to indicate chords as in section D above. If a chord is used more than once in a measure, you need not name each appearance. Ignore circled notes in your analysis.

Measure 4 _____

Measure 5 _____

Measure 6 _____

Measure 7 _____

Measure 8 _____

Measure 9 _____

Measure 10 _____

D. Refer to Mason's "Joy to the World" on page 225.
   1. Ignore circled notes that are not a part of the chords.
   2. Write a Roman numeral analysis and indicate the position:

   ^{6} —if chord is in first inversion

   $^6_4$ —if chord is in second inversion

   no numbers—if chord is in root position

E. The following are four-part arrangements of triads.
   1. On the staff below each chord, write out the triad in root position (see the example).
   2. In the first blank, write the type of triad (M = major, m = minor, d = diminished, A = augmented) using the symbols shown in part A (above).
   3. In the lower blank, write the sign indicating the arrangement of the four-part harmony:

   ^{6} —if chord is in first inversion

   $^6_4$ —if chord is in second inversion

   no numbers—if chord is in root position

The Fundamentals of Music

Name _____

Section _____

Date _____

F. Here is an excerpt from a piano composition. Instead of being written in block chords, as in part E, the harmony is arpeggiated (spread out in a linear fashion).

1. In each blank, write the chord analysis using Roman numerals (as shown on pages 71-73 of the text). The following chords are used:

$$V \qquad iv^6 \qquad i^6_4 \qquad ii°^6 \qquad V^6 \qquad iv^6_4 \qquad i$$

2. Note that there is one chord per measure until measure 7, which contains three chords.

G.   Complete each chord according to figured bass symbols. Use the simple position (the closest possible arrangement).

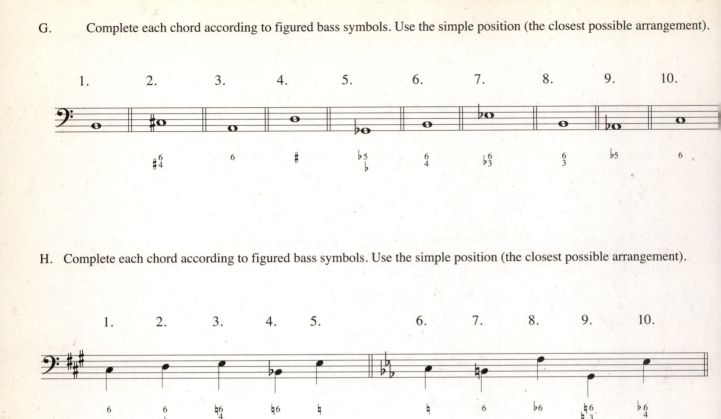

H. Complete each chord according to figured bass symbols. Use the simple position (the closest possible arrangement).

Review

1. Take a single note. Spell one major, one minor, one augmented, and one diminished triad with that note as the root. Now make that note the third of each of the four triad qualities. Now make it the fifth of each triad quality. Choose another note and repeat the exercise.
2. Review the concepts listed at the beginning of the chapter in the text.
3. Choose a note and write the major scale and then a triad on each scale degree. Identify the quality of each triad and write the appropriate Roman numeral below the chord. Repeat this exercise using the natural minor scale, the harmonic minor scale, and the melodic minor scale. Repeat this exercise using a different note.
4. Take a familiar hymn or look at the "Hallelujah" chorus from Handel's *Messiah* on page 207 in the anthology. Examine the notes in the four parts on a given beat and identify a chord, if possible (there may be tones that are not part of the chords in this music, so don't be surprised if you can't always identify a chord). Identify the inversion for each chord you find.
5. Use computer software if it is available.

Test Yourself 4

Answers are on page 163.

1. Indicate the quality (major, minor, augmented, diminished) of each of the following triads:

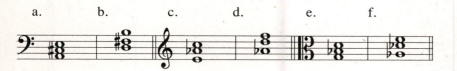

   a.   b.   c.   d.   e.   f.

2. Give the popular music chord symbol for each of the triads above.

3. For each of the following chords, name the scale degree on which it is built, and give the correct Roman numeral. Indicate the inversions in the standard way.

   a.   b.   c.   d.   e.   f.   g.   h.   i.

B♭M:

4. Indicate the proper Roman numeral for the given chord if it occurs in each of the following keys:

   a. A-flat major   b. G minor   c. B-flat major
   d. C minor   e. E-flat major   f. F minor

5. Indicate the proper Roman numeral for the given chord if it occurs in each of the following keys:

   a. D major   b. F-sharp minor   c. A major
   d. E minor   e. G major   f. B minor

Chords   **31**

5 Cadences and Nonharmonic Tones

Name _____

Section _____

Date _____

A. Refer to Nicolai's *Wachet auf, ruft uns die Stimme* on page 235. Each phrase ending is marked with a fermata and the key is indicated just before the cadence. Name the cadence of each phrase using the following list of cadence types:

Imperfect Authentic   Plagal
Perfect Authentic   Deceptive
Half

Measure Numbers	Cadence
4–5	_____
9–10	_____
13–14	_____
17–18	_____
20–21	_____
23–24	_____
25–26	_____
27–28	_____
31–32	_____

B. Rewrite each chord progression in the blank provided and add the requested nonharmonic tone.

1. Passing tone
2. Accented passing tone
3. Neighboring tone
4. Anticipation in soprano

5. Appoggiatura in soprano
6. 4–3 suspension
7. 7–6 suspension
8. Escape tone in soprano

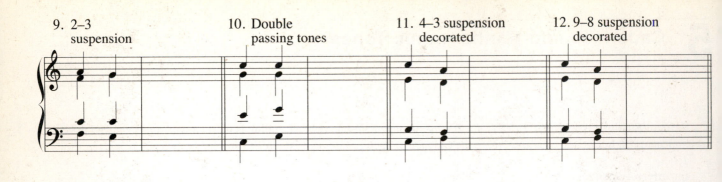

9. 2–3 suspension   10. Double passing tones   11. 4–3 suspension decorated   12. 9–8 suspension decorated

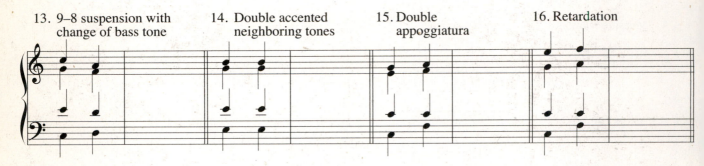

13. 9–8 suspension with change of bass tone   14. Double accented neighboring tones   15. Double appoggiatura   16. Retardation

C. Following are two phrases of a chorale harmonized by Bach. The nonharmonic tones (except for three) have been removed.
1. Provide a Roman numeral harmonic analysis of each chord (except the one marked X), indicating also the position (root position, first inversion, and so on).
2. Then, in the blank staves, rewrite the two phrases and add nonharmonic tones of your choice. Include at least two suspensions. If you wish to add escape tones, anticipations, or appoggiaturas, place them *only* in the soprano voice. Other nonharmonic tones can be added to any voice.

Vater unser im Himmelreich (Our Father, Thou in Heaven Above),
BWV 102, m. 1–2, 11–12.

____ : __ __ __ __
(Key)

____ : __ __ __ __ __ __ X __ __ __
(Key)   (vii°⁷/V)

D. The following are examples of Bach chorales.
1. Write the Roman numeral analysis of each chord and indicate the position— ^{6} if in first inversion, $^6_4$ if in second inversion, and no numbers if in root position.
2. Circle all nonharmonic tones and write the abbreviations representing the name nearby.

$$\begin{array}{rcl}
\text{Unaccented passing tone} & = & \text{PT} \\
\text{Accented passing tone} & = & \text{PT} \\
\text{9–8 suspension} & = & \text{9–8 sus} \\
\text{2–3 suspension} & = & \text{2–3 sus}
\end{array}$$

The first chord of each example is analyzed correctly for you.

1. *Lobt Gott, ihr Christen, allzugleich* (Praise God, Ye Christians, All Together), BWV 376, m. 1–2.

AM: I

2. *Wo soll ich fliehen hin* (Whither Am I to Flee),
   BWV 89, m. 1–2.

gm: i

3. *Christe, du Beistand deiner Kreuzgemeine* (Christ, Thou
   Support of Thy Followers), BWV 275, m. 1–2.

dm: i

4. *Liebster Jesu, wir sind hier* (Dearest Jesus, We Are Here),
   BWV 373, m. 1–2.

GM: I

5. *Seelen-Braütigam* (Bridegroom of the Soul),
   BWV 409, m. 1–2.

AM: I

Name _____

Section _____

Date _____

E. Refer to the chorale *Werde munter, mein Gemüte*, harmonized by Johann Sebastian Bach (1685–1750) on page 183.
   1. Add the Roman numeral analysis of each chord. Include also the proper designation for chord position (root position, first inversion, second inversion, and so on).
   2. Write the initials representing each nonharmonic device above or below the particular tone.

F. Following are ten excerpts, most of which are taken from chorales harmonized by Johann Sebastian Bach.
   1. Write the analysis of each chord in the blank below the staves.
   2. Remember, if a triad contains a nonharmonic tone, analyze it as if the nonharmonic tone were not present— mentally replace the nonharmonic tone with the corresponding chord tone (see no. 6).
   3. Circle each nonharmonic tone.
   4. Place the number representing the nonharmonic tone near the circle (see list that follows).
   5. In these examples most of the nonharmonic tones will be of eighth-note value, but be careful not to overlook those of quarter-note value as well (see no. 6).
   6. Note that the excerpts contain little more than a measure and are not to be considered complete musical ideas.

Nonharmonic Tone Types

1. 9–8 suspension	8. Escape tone
2. 7–6 suspension	9. Changing tones
3. 4–3 suspension	10. Anticipation
4. 2–3 suspension	11. Double unaccented passing tones
5. Unaccented passing tone	12. Lower neighboring tone
6. Accented passing tone	13. Upper neighboring tone
7. Appoggiatura	14. Double lower neighboring tones

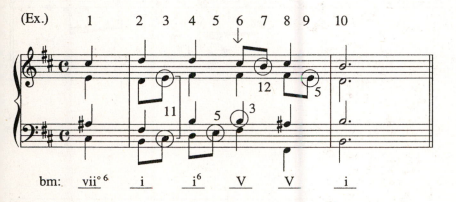

(Key)   (Key)

3.

4.

(Key) : _____ _____ _____ _____   (Key) : _____ _____ _____ _____

5.

6.

(Key) : _____ _____ _____ _____   (Key) : _____ _____ _____ _____

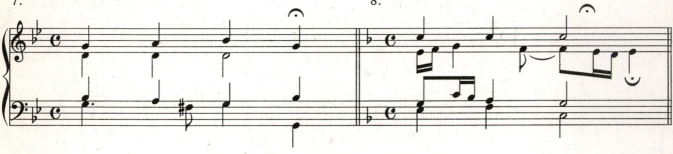

7.

8.

(Key) : _____ _____ _____ _____   (Key) : _____ _____ _____ _____

9.

10.

(Key) : _____ _____ _____ _____   (Key) : _____ _____ _____ _____

Review

1. Play all the examples of cadences (figures 5.1–5.4 on pages 90–91 in the text) on the piano and identify the features of each cadence as described in the accompanying text. Even if your piano skills are minimal, you will find this to be a helpful exercise.
2. Choose a few pieces from a collection of traditional and patriotic songs, a hymnal, or some similar music with clear phrases and a text.
   a. Find the key of each piece.
   b. Identify phrases by the given punctuation marks in the text.
   c. For each phrase identify the cadence type (authentic, plagal, etc.). Some phrases may be in keys other than the key of the piece as a whole, and you may not be able to identify the cadence type in every case.
   d. Examine the length of the phrases. Are all phrases the same length?
3. Look over the assignments you have completed for this chapter, paying particular attention to any difficulties you have encountered. Think through the process for completing each exercise.
4. Since you are likely to find problems similar to the assignments on an examination, work through some of the assignments that you were not required to complete during your study of the chapter. This will give you practice in working with the concepts of the chapter.
5. Play the examples of nonharmonic tones (figures 5.8–5.25 on pages 93–99 of the text) on the piano. Pay particular attention to the three-tone pattern: *preceding tone, nonharmonic tone, and following tone.*
6. Study the summary of nonharmonic tones on page 100 of the text and memorize the approach and departure characteristics of each. Also memorize the list of abbreviations at the top of the chart. You will need these abbreviations to label nonharmonic tones in assignments and examinations.
7. Review the fundamentals (chapters 1–5). You must review these basic facts on a regular basis and practice to achieve fluency. This repeated review will pay big dividends in future chapters.

Test Yourself 5

Answers are on page 164.

Name the cadence type in the following short excerpts (each ending with a cadence). The cadence types are:

Imperfect Authentic	Plagal
Perfect Authentic	Deceptive
Half	

1. _____   2. _____   3. _____

dm: GM: cm:

*Occasionally a 5th is missing. In this instance analyze as if the 5th ("B") were present.

Name _____

Section _____

Date _____

16._____ 17._____ 18._____

B♭M: fm: AM:

19._____ 20._____ 21._____

em: gm: bm:

22._____ 23._____ 24._____

EM: gm: E♭M:

Questions 25 and 26 refer to these examples:

25. Cadences:
    a. The cadence at chord 3 is a(n) _____ cadence.
    b. The cadence at chord 6 is a(n) _____ cadence.
    c. The cadence at chord 9 is a(n) _____ cadence.
    d. The cadence at chord 12 is a(n) _____ cadence.
    e. The cadence at chord 15 is a(n) _____ cadence.

26. Nonharmonic tones:
    a. The nonharmonic tone at chord 2 is a(n) _____.
    b. The nonharmonic tone at chord 5 is a(n) _____.
    c. The nonharmonic tone at chord 8 is a(n) _____.
    d. The nonharmonic tone at chord 9 is a(n) _____.
    e. The nonharmonic tone at chord 11 is a(n) _____.
    f. The nonharmonic tone at chord 13 is a(n) _____.
    g. The nonharmonic tone at chord 14 is a(n) _____.

6 Melodic Organization

A. Following are 10 themes from symphonies by or attributed to Franz Joseph Haydn. Some are based on a motive and some are not.
1. Analyze each theme.
2. If the theme is based on a motive, circle the motive and each recurrence. Remember, a *motive* is a short melodic-rhythmic figure of just a few notes that is repeated (sometimes with modifications) enough times for the listener to be aware of its existence.
3. If the theme is not based on a motive, write "no" at the end of the score.

1. Symphony No. 103 (Drum Roll), Hob. I:103 in E-flat Major, II, m. 1–4.

2. Symphony No. 104 (London), Hob. I:104 in D Major, I, m. 17–20.

3. Symphony No. 104 (London), Hob. I:104 in D Major, II (Andante), m. 1–4.

4. Symphony No. 104 (London), Hob. I:104 in D Major, IV (Finale), m. 3–8.

5. Symphony in C Major (Toy) (attributed to Haydn).

6. Symphony in C Major (Toy) (attributed to Haydn).

7. Symphony in C Major (Toy) (attributed to Haydn).

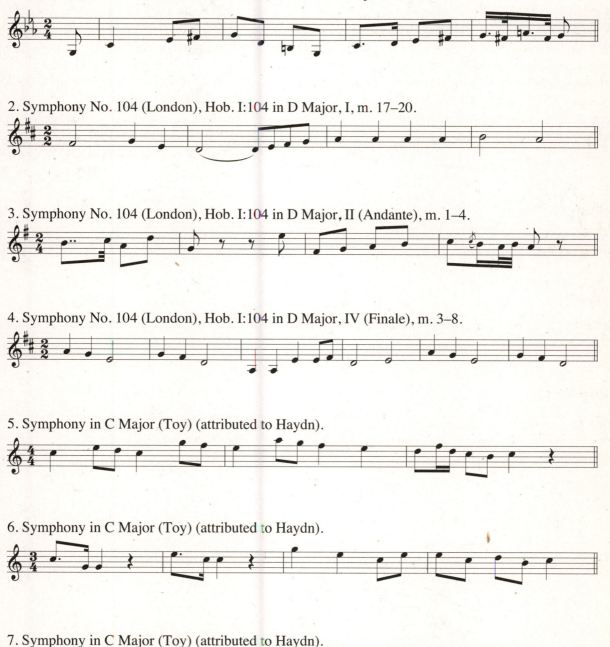

8. Symphony in C Major (Toy) (attributed to Haydn).

9. Symphony No. 101 (Clock), Hob. I:101 in D Major, III (Menuet), m. 1–8.

10. Symphony No. 101 (Clock), Hob. I:101 in D Major, IV (Finale), m. 1–4.

B.   Below are three phrases. Using the phrase relationships requested, add an additional phrase to each to make a period.

Modified repeated:

Parallel:

Contrasting:

Modified repeated:

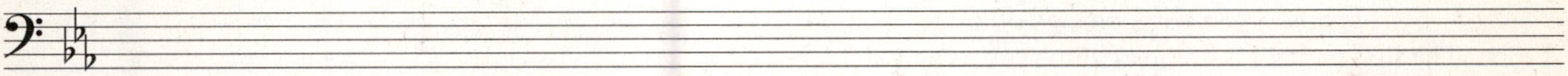

Parallel:

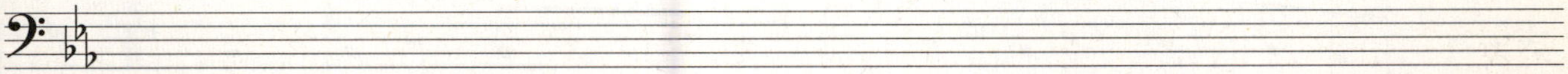

Contrasting:

Tonality of D:

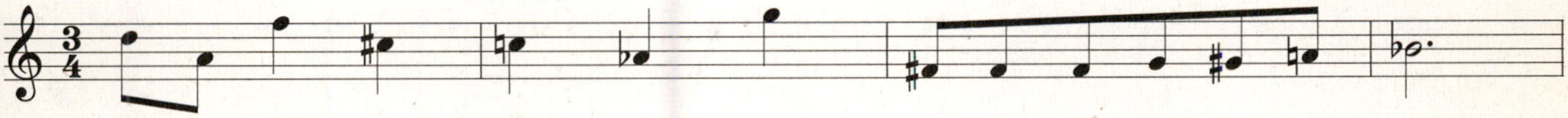

Modified repeated:

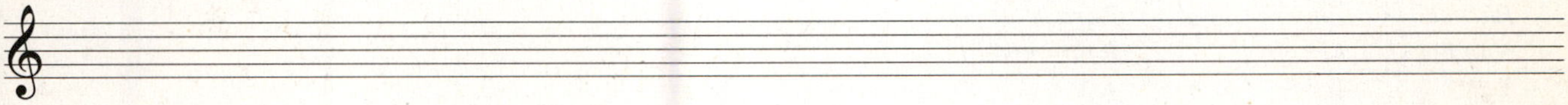

Parallel:

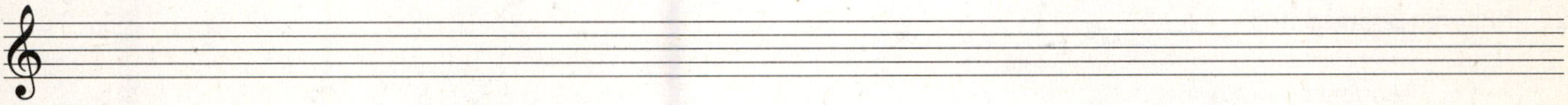

Contrasting:

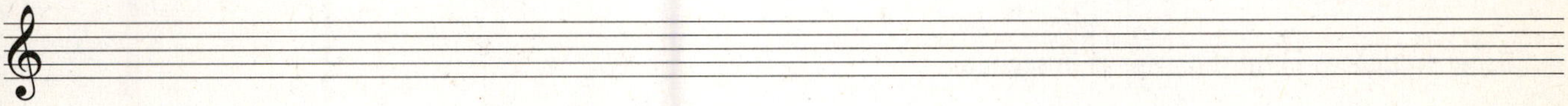

C. Following are six melodies. Study each carefully and indicate the following.
   1.   A *phrase diagram*. Give the length of each phrase and its relationship to other phrases.
        A = The first phrase and any that are an exact repetition.
        A' = Any subsequent phrase that is a modified repeated version of the first phrase.
       AP = A phrase following A that is in parallel relationship to it.
        B = The next phrase after A that is contrasting to it (and any later phrases that are an exact repetition of B).
        B' = Any subsequent phrase that is a modified repeated version of the B phrase.
       BP = A phrase following B that is in parallel relationship to it.
        Continue this procedure through C, D, E, and so on, as needed.
   2.   Point out any melodic organization you find, such as:

        sequence   extension of a phrase
        motive   compression of a phrase
        phrase member   change of mode

   3.   The first melody is completed for you as a model.

(Ex.) Beethoven: Sonata in C Minor *(Pathétique),* op. 13, III (Rondo), m. 1–12.

1. Phrase diagram:

Phrase Number	Phrase Length	Phrase Relationship
1	1–15	A
2	18–31	B
3	32–45	B

2. Melodic organization:

3–4 is a sequence with 5–6
9–10 is a sequence with 11–12
18–21 is a sequence with 22–25
27–28 is a sequence with 29–30

Same sequences in third phrase as in second.

Phrase member: 1–7
Phrase member: 9–15

Motive 18–19 appears ten times in phrases 2 and 3.

1. Schubert: Sonata in A Major, D. 959, III (Rondo), m. 1–16.

1. Phrase diagram (follow the model):

2. Melodic organization:

2. Schubert: Sonata in C Minor, D. 958, III (Allegro), m. 1–16 (transposed and adapted).

1. Phrase diagram (follow the model):

2. Melodic organization:

3. Haydn: Allegro.

1. Phrase diagram (follow the model):

2. Melodic organization:

4. Allegretto (England).

1. Phrase diagram (follow the model):

2. Melodic organization:

The Structural Elements of Music

5. Andante con Moto (Spain).

1. Phrase diagram (follow the model):

2. Melodic organization:

6. Moderato (England).

1. Phrase diagram (follow the model):

2. Melodic organization:

The Structural Elements of Music

D. Expand the following phrase in the three ways requested.

Expansion at the beginning:

Internal expansion:

Cadential expansion:

E. Add a phrase with change in mode to the following phrase by Mozart.

Mozart: Symphony in G Minor, K. 183, III (Trio).

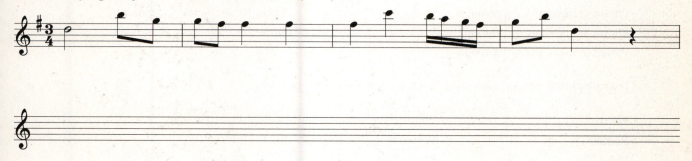

F. Make this two-measure melody into a four-measure phrase with a diatonic sequence.

G. Add a sequence segment to this two-measure melody. The added segment should be in C melodic minor and should end with an implied perfect authentic cadence (in C minor).

H. Add a sequence segment to this two-measure melody. The added segment should be in F major and should end with a perfect authentic cadence (in F major).

I. Continue this two-measure melody with a false sequence of two measures.

J. Refer to the Menuet from the Sonata in A Major by Haydn on page 217.
    1 . Considering only the melody (highest voice), divide the composition into phrases. (Indications for eleven phrases are provided below, but alternate analyses may specify fewer.)

    Phrase 1: measures ____ through ____   Phrase 7: measures ____ through ____
    Phrase 2: measures ____ through ____   Phrase 8: measures ____ through ____
    Phrase 3: measures ____ through ____   Phrase 9: measures ____ through ____
    Phrase 4: measures ____ through ____   Phrase 10: measures ____ through ____
    Phrase 5: measures ____ through ____   Phrase 11: measures ____ through ____
    Phrase 6: measures ____ through ____

    2. Indicate phrase relationships using letters as described in the text.

    Phrase 1 ____   Phrase 5 ____   Phrase 9 ____
    Phrase 2 ____   Phrase 6 ____   Phrase 10 ____
    Phrase 3 ____   Phrase 7 ____   Phrase 11 ____
    Phrase 4 ____   Phrase 8 ____

    3. Indicate melodic repetitions (Use measure numbers.)

    _____   _____

    _____   _____

4. Indicate melodic sequences. (Use measure numbers and name the types of sequences.)

_____   _____

_____   _____

_____   _____

_____   _____

_____   _____

5. Considering the melodic line only, indicate the key of each bracketed section.

Bracket 1 ___   Bracket 4 ___   Bracket 7 ___

Bracket 2 ___   Bracket 5 ___   Bracket 8 ___

Bracket 3 ___   Bracket 6 ___

K. Following are twelve excerpts from compositions. Analyze each melody in the following manner:

1. Indicate the *climax tone* with a box:

2. Indicate *ascent* pitches with an ascending line:

3. Show *descent* pitches with a descending line:

4. Circle notes of the tonic triad:

5. Number the scale pitches that conclude the phrase or period. Remember that scale degrees $\hat{3}$ and $\hat{2}$ must occur in that order but may be scattered throughout the excerpt, while $\hat{1}$ is always the final pitch of the phrase or period.

(Ex.) British Folk Song.

E♭M:

1. England.

Allegro

bᵇm:

2. Monk: "Abide with Me" (hymn tune).

CM:

3. Schubert: Impromptu, op. 142, no. 2, D. 935.

AᵇM:

4. Verdi: Aïda, Act II, Scene II (March), m. 91–94.

AᵇM:

5. Schubert: *Das Wandern* (The Wandering) from *Die Schöne Müllerin* (The Miller's Beautiful Daughter), op. 25, no. 1, D. 795, m. 5–7.

BᵇM:

6. Schubert: Waltz, op. 9, no. 8, D. 365.

AᵇM:

Name _____

Section _____

Date _____

7. Mozart: Magic Flute, Act I, no. 8 (Finale), m. 303–310.

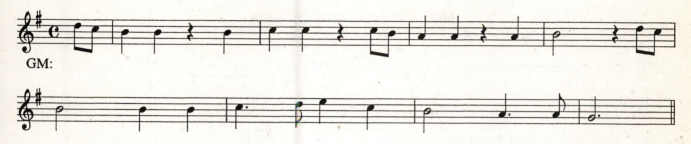

GM:

8. Mendelssohn: *Ein Sommernachtstraum* (A Midsummer Night's Dream), op. 21, no. 5 (Allegro molto comodo), m. 148–155.

AM:

9. Russian Folk Song.

GM:

10. German Folk Song.

E♭M:

11. Mozart: Rondo.

CM:

12. Harrison: In the Gloaming.

FM:

Review

1. This chapter introduces many terms that are used to describe the structure and organization of melody. Use the list of terms at the beginning of the chapter (page 109 of the text) as the basis for your review. Define each term for yourself and then check your definition with the appropriate section of the chapter.
2. Carefully examine the melodies that are given as examples in the chapter. Play or sing each melody and observe the labels applied to it.
3. Choose a few pieces from a collection of traditional and patriotic songs, a hymnal, or some similar music with clear phrases and a text.
    a. Find the key of each piece.
    b. Identify phrases by the given punctuation marks in the text.
    c. For each phrase identify the cadence type (authentic, plagal, etc.). Some phrases may be in keys other than the key of the piece as a whole, and you may not be able to identify the cadence type in every case.
    d. Examine the length of the phrases. Are all phrases the same length?
    e. Are the phrases grouped together into periods? How do you know? Are the periods parallel, contrasting, three-phrase, or double? How can you tell?
    f. Does the melody contain repeated melodic motives?
4. Look at music you are currently learning or that you have learned in the past. See if you can find an example of each of the elements of melody in the list at the beginning of the chapter.

Test Yourself 6

Answers are on page 165.

Following is an excerpt from a rondo by Wolfgang Amadeus Mozart (1756–91). A list of terms denoting compositional and formal devices follows it.

   Examine the rondo carefully and locate an example of each of the terms listed. Then indicate the place in the composition where the example is found, using the line letters and beat numbers. (An example is provided.)

Mozart: Rondo K. 494.

Line E

Term	Line(s)	Can Be Found in Number(s)
1. (Ex.) Internal extension of a phrase	A	5-8 and 9-12
2. Parallel period	_____	_____
3. A sequence of two segments of one-half measure each	_____	_____
4. A retardation	_____	_____
5. An appoggiatura	_____	_____
6. A 4–3 suspension	_____	_____
7. A sequence of two segments of one full measure each	_____	_____
8. An authentic cadence in F major	_____	_____
9. A half cadence in C major	_____	_____
10. Exact melodic repetition	_____	_____
11. A 7–6 suspension	_____	_____
12. A lower neighboring tone	_____	_____
13. An accented passing tone	_____	_____
14. A second-inversion triad	_____	_____
15. An imperfect authentic cadence in C major	_____	_____
16. A phrase member	_____	_____
17. A phrase extension near the beginning	_____	_____
18. A set of contrasting phrases (period)	_____	_____

Questions 19–21 refer to the "Lullaby" by Brahms:

Brahms: "Lullaby," op. 49, no. 4.

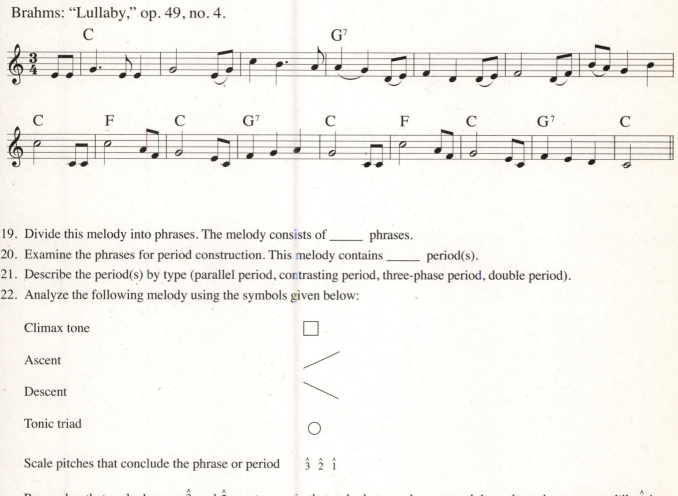

19. Divide this melody into phrases. The melody consists of _____ phrases.

20. Examine the phrases for period construction. This melody contains _____ period(s).

21. Describe the period(s) by type (parallel period, contrasting period, three-phase period, double period).

22. Analyze the following melody using the symbols given below:

Climax tone   ☐

Ascent   ╱

Descent   ╲

Tonic triad   ◯

Scale pitches that conclude the phrase or period $\hat{3}$ $\hat{2}$ $\hat{1}$

Remember that scale degrees $\hat{3}$ and $\hat{2}$ must occur in that order but may be scattered throughout the excerpt, while $\hat{1}$ is always the final pitch of the phrase or period.

German Folk Song.

7 Texture and Textural Reduction

Name _____

Section _____

Date _____

A. Refer to Beethoven's Sonata in E-flat Major, op. 31, no. 3, on page 187.
   1. Examine the opening section of this work (measures 1–9A).
   2. The texture type is _____.
   3. Label the elements of the texture in measures 1–9A using the following labels:

   PM = Primary melody
   SM = Secondary melody
   PSM = Parallel supporting melody
   SS = Static support
   RS = Rhythmic support
   HRS = Harmonic and rhythmic support

B. Refer to Handel's Gigue from Harpsichord Suite no. 7 in B-flat Major, on page 205.
   1. The texture type is _____.
   2. Label the elements of the texture throughout the composition using the labels in section A above.

C. Refer to Mozart's Piano Sonata in A Major, K 331, on page 231.
   1. Examine measures 1–8 and identify the texture type. The texture is _____.
   2. Label the elements in the texture in measures 1–8 using the labels in section A above.

D. Refer to Schumann's *Davidsbündlertänze* op. 6, no. 8 on page 236.
   1. Examine measures 1–7 and identify the texture type. The texture is _____.
   2. Label the elements in the texture in measures 1–7 using the labels in section A above.
   3. How does the texture of the following section (measures 8–14) differ from the first section?

E. Refer to Handel's "Hallelujah!" from *Messiah,* on page 207.
   1. This work exhibits several texture types. Examine the sections listed below and identify the texture type of each section.

	Texture Type
Measures 4–11	_____
Measures 12–14	_____
Measures 22–32	_____
Measures 33–41	_____
Measures 41–43	_____
Measures 69–73	_____
Measures 90–94	_____

   2. Do a textural analysis of the entire work, using the labels in section A above.

F. Refer to Beethoven's String Quartet in C minor, op. 18, no. 4, on page 191.
   1. This short work is divided into four repeated sections and each section has a characteristic texture. Describe the texture of each section by type and summarize the results of a textural analysis. The first section (measures 1–8) is completed as an example.

(Ex.) Section I:

      The texture in this section is homophonic with the PM in the first violin and RHS in the other three instruments.

Section II (measures 9–17)

Section III (measures 18–26)

Section IV (measures 27–42)

G. Refer to Haydn's Sonata in E Minor, Hob. XVI:34, on page 220.
    1. Determine the harmonic rhythm by playing the piece or listening to a recording.
    2. Do a harmonic reduction of the left hand (there are no nonharmonic tones until measure 15) and write the chords on the staff provided. Make sure to use proper rhythmic values.

Review

1. The four basic texture types and the seven textural elements are the most important concepts of this chapter. Review the discussion of each of these concepts, paying careful attention to the musical examples. In the discussion of textural elements (pages 136–140 in the text) the examples are analyzed. Carefully examine the labels and see if you understand the reason for each.

2. You should begin to look at the music you are performing to determine the texture type and relationship of textural elements. If you play a "one-line" instrument, this may be somewhat difficult, but you can use your ears or examine scores. You will find it very helpful to know how the lines you play fit into the texture. In many cases this information will assist you in interpretation. For instance, this information will alert you to bring out your part when it is the primary melody (PM), or to subordinate it when it is a secondary melody (SM) or a part of harmonic and rhythmic support (HRS).

3. The technique of harmonic reduction of accompaniment figures described on pages 140–142 of the text will be extremely valuable to you in later musical analysis in this class. Practice this technique, using the examples in the text, the assignments, and compositions in the anthology section of this workbook. The following passages in the anthology will give you additional practice:

Beethoven: Sonata in E-Flat, op. 31, no. 3, III, m. 25–32 (pages 187–190).

Kuhlau: Sonatina in F, op. 55, no. 4, II, m. 9–16 (pages 223–224).

Mozart: *Eine kleine Nachtmusik,* K. 525, III, m. 17–24 (pages 226–228). (See keyboard reduction of this piece on page 324 of the textbook.)

Test Yourself 7

Answers are on page 166.

Questions 1–4 refer to the four musical excerpts below.

1. Examine the four excerpts, which contain the four basic texture types described in the chapter. Identify the texture types and fill in the blanks below:

      monophonic texture _____.

      polyphonic texture _____.

      homophonic texture _____.

      homorhythmic texture _____.

2. Each excerpt has one or more parts labeled with numbers (1–7). Identify the textural elements and fill in the blanks below (you won't find an example of every textural element):

Primary melody (PM) _____.

Secondary melody (SM) _____.

Parallel supporting melody (PSM) _____.

Static support (SS) _____.

Harmonic support (HS) _____.

Rhythmic support (RS) _____.

Harmonic rhythmic support (HRS) _____.

3. The thinnest texture is example _____.

4. The thickest texture is example _____.

a. Morley: "Sing We and Chant It," m. 9–16.

b. Handel: *Messiah*, II ("Comfort Ye"), m. 15–19.

com - fort -a - bly to Je - ru - sa - lem,

c. Haydn: Quartet, op. 76, no. 3, II (poco adagio), m. 20–24.

d. Debussy: Prelude to *The Afternoon of a Faun,* m. 1–4.

5. Write a harmonic reduction for the bass clef (left-hand) portion of the following excerpt. The harmonic rhythm is given and nonharmonic tones have been circled.

Beethoven: Sonata, op. 13, III (Allegro), m. 1–8.

6. The right hand part in the preceding example is _____ (textural element). The left-hand part is _____ (textural element). The excerpt is an example of _____ texture (texture type).

Voice Leading in Two Voices

A. On the following pages are six examples of *cantus firmus* melodies.
   1. Compose a counterpoint above each *cantus firmus* using the principles in chapter 8.
   2. Compose a counterpoint below each *cantus firmus* using the principles in chapter 8.
   3. Pay particular attention to proper beginnings and endings, as shown on pages 152–153 of the text.
   4. Make sure your counterpoint observes all the principles on pages 153–154 of the text.
   5. Fill in the intervals between your counterpoints and the *cantus firmus* in the blanks provided.

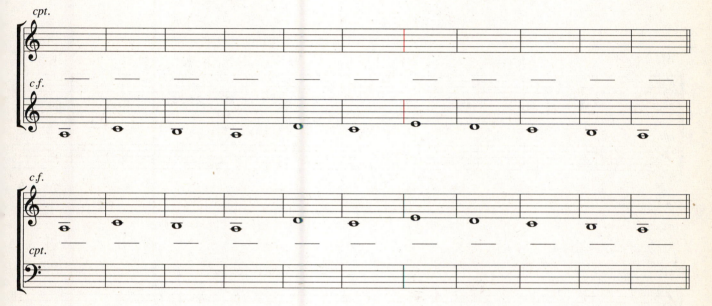

The Structural Elements of Music

Review

1. Study the examples of first species counterpoint on page 156 of the text. For each pair of tones in the counterpoint determine which of the basic principles on pages 153–154 is being used.
2. Examine each counterpoint in terms of the eleven melodic guides on pages 155–156.
3. Examine each counterpoint, keeping in mind the three guides related to relationships between two voices (page 156, numbers 12–14).
4. Since voice leading is a skill that you must learn by practice, the best way to review this chapter is to compose additional counterpoints above and below each *cantus firmus*. Your instructor may provide you with additional examples for practice.

Test Yourself 8

Answers on page 167.

Below are four examples of first species counterpoint. In each case there are several violations of the principles of first species counterpoint. Fill in the intervals between the *cantus firmus* and the counterpoint in the blanks provided. Examine each example and note all violations of good voice leading practice.

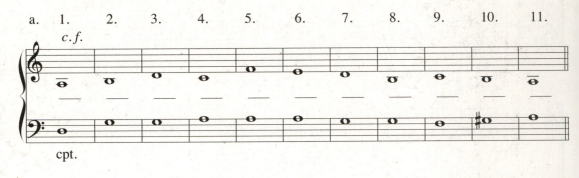

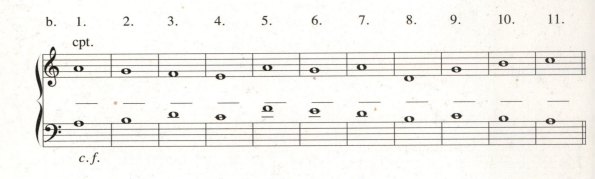

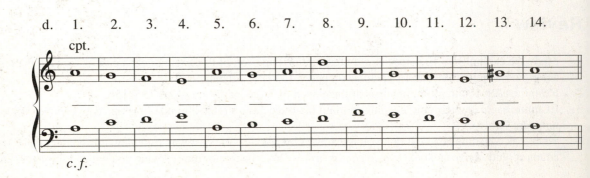

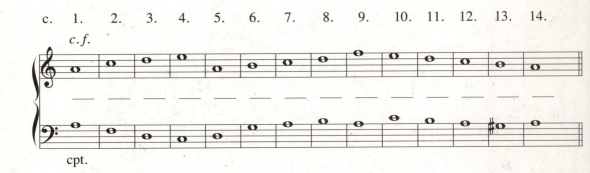

9 Voice Leading in Four Voices

Name _____

Section _____

Date _____

A. Following are five harmonized chorale phrases. Each phrase contains errors in part writing. On a separate sheet of paper, list the errors in each phrase. (The chords are numbered for easy identification.)

To refresh your memory, here are a number of common errors in four-voice writing.

1. Parallel 5ths, octaves, or unison are to be avoided.
2. Never double the leading tone of the scale.
3. Keep each of the four voices within its range.
4. Avoid the *augmented 2nd* and the *augmented 4th* in the melodic line of any of the four voices.
5. *Root* should be doubled when triad is in root position (first choice).
6. *Soprano voice* should be doubled when major or minor triads are in 1st inversion (first choice).
7. *Bass note* should be doubled when diminished triads are in 1st inversion. The root positions of diminished triads are seldom found.
8. All factors of triads should be present.
9. Avoid large leaps of a 6th or more. Octave leaps are an exception.
10. Maintain an *octave or less* between soprano and alto and between alto and tenor voices.

1. *Jesu, meine Zuversicht* (Jesus, My Sure Defense).

2. *Als Jesus Christus in der Nacht* (As Jesus was Betrayed in the Night).

3. *Christ lag in Todesbanden* (Christ Lay in the Bonds of Death).

4. *Komm, Gott, Schöpfer, Heiliger Geist* (Come God, Creator, Holy Ghost).

5. *Christus, der uns selig macht* (Christ Who Makes Us Holy).

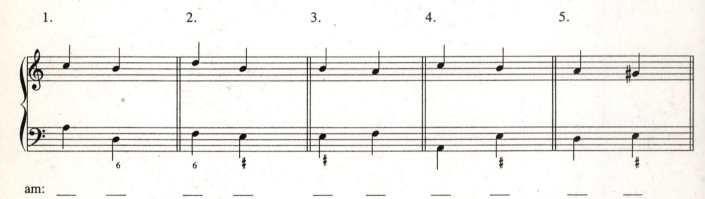

B. Each of the following exercises consists of a single progression.
1. Add the alto and tenor voices to these progressions.
2. Observe traditional part-writing practices as enumerated in the text.
3. In the blanks below the staves, provide a complete harmonic analysis of each chord.

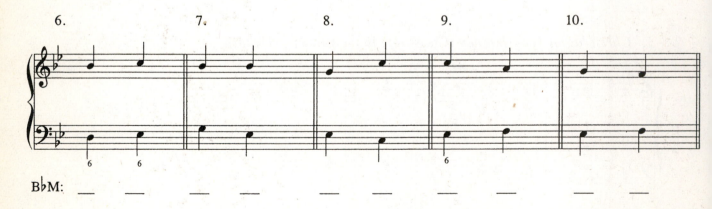

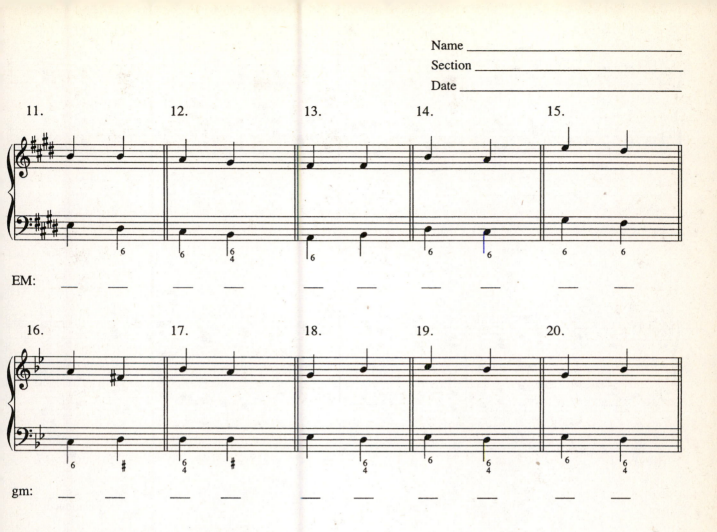

C. Below are six harmonized chorale phrases.
1. Analyze each chord using Roman numerals and indications for inversions.
2. Circle all nonharmonic tones and indicate the type by using the abbreviations in the list that follows.
3. Name the cadence type that concludes each phrase.

Nonharmonic Tones

PT = Unaccented passing tone

$\overset{>}{PT}$ = Accented passing tone

NT = Neighboring tone

7–6 SUS = 7–6 suspension

4–3 SUS = 4–3 suspension

| (Key) | 1 | 2 | 3 | 4 | 5 | 6 | 7 | (Key) | 1 | 2 | 3 | 4 | 5 | 6 | 7 |

Cadence   Cadence

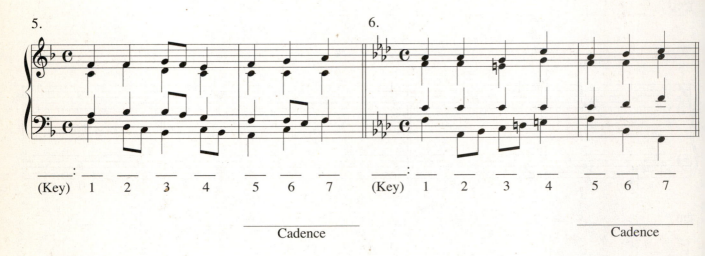

| (Key) | 1 | 2 | 3 | 4 | 5 | 6 | 7 | (Key) | 1 | 2 | 3 | 4 | 5 | 6 | 7 |

Cadence   Cadence

D. Following are eight chorale phrases that have been harmonized by Bach.
1. Make a complete harmonic analysis of each phrase, including Roman numerals and indications for inversions.
2. Circle each nonharmonic tone and, using the abbreviations listed below, indicate its type.

PT = Unaccented passing tone
P̆T = Accented passing tone
NT = Neighboring tone
9–8 SUS = 9–8 suspension
4–3 SUS = 4–3 suspension

1. *Wie schön leuchtet der Morgenstern*
   (How Brightly Shines the Morning Star),
   BWV 172, m. 1–2.

2. *Ermuntre dich, mein schwacher Geist*
   (Rouse Thyself, My Weak Spirit),
   BWV 43, m. 5–8.

| (Key) | 1 | 2 | 3 | 4 | 5 | 6 | 7 | 8 | 9 | (Key) | 1 | 2 | 3 | 4 | 5 | 6 | 7 |

3. *Alle Menschen müssen sterben*
   (All Men Must Die),
   BWV 262, m. 1–2.

4. *Wer weiss, wie nahe mir mein Ende*
   (Who Knows How Near My End May Be),
   BWV 166, m. 1–2.

(Key) 1 2 3 4 5 6 7 8   (Key) 1 2 3 4 5 6 7 8

5. *Es ist gewisslich an der Zeit*
   (It Is Certainly Time),
   BWV 307, m. 1–2.

6. *Wer nur den lieben Gott lässt walten*
   (He Who Lets Only Beloved God Rule),
   BWV 197, m. 1–3.

(Key) 1 2 3 4 5 6 7 8   (Key) 1 2 3 4 5 6 7 8 9

7. *Vater unser im Himmelreich*
   (Our Father, Who Art in Heaven),
   BWV 102, m. 1–2.

8. *Herzlich lieb hab ich dich, o Herr*
   (I Love Thee Dearly, O Lord),
   BWV 340, m. 1–2.

(Key) 1 2 3 4 5 6 7 8 9   (Key) 1 2 3 4 5 6 7 8

E. Each exercise consists of a chorale phrase.
  1. Add the alto and tenor voices according to the figured bass symbols.
  2. Observe traditional part-writing practices as given in the text.
  3. In the blanks below the staves, provide a complete harmonic analysis of each chord.

1. Alternate doubling of soprano and bass in successive triads in 1st inversion.
2. Double 3rd of VI triad to avoid augmented 2nd in alto voice. The vi and VI triads almost always receive this treatment when preceded by V.
3. The E-natural is a result of the melodic minor scale.
4. Double 6th above bass note here. Doubling soprano will create parallel octaves, and doubling the bass note doubles the leading tone of the scale.

6.

5   5

6   6   6   6

___ : ___ ___ ___ ___ ___ ___ ___
(Key)

7.

5

6   6

___ : ___ ___ ___ ___ ___ ___ ___
(Key)

8.

6   6

___ : ___ ___ ___ ___ ___ ___ ___ ___
(Key)

5.   Investigate the possibility of unequal 5ths here (perfect to diminished or vice versa). Are alternatives possible?

F.   Following is an excerpt from a *trio sonata,* one of the most important types of composition in the baroque period. A trio sonata consists of two upper parts (usually taken by violins, flutes, and so on) and a lower part that includes a figured bass. A gambist (performer on the viola da gamba) or cellist plays the lower line while a harpsichordist or pianist *realizes* the continuo part (plays the chords requested by the figured bass).

Write out the tenor and alto parts of the continuo according to the figured bass symbols. Observe traditional part-writing procedures as indicated in the text.

Vivaldi: *Sonata Da Camera a Tre* (Chamber Sonata for Three) in D Minor.

G. The following chorales, harmonized by Bach, may be used for further analysis and study:
   O Herre Gott, dein göttlich Wort (page 179)
   Gottes Sohn ist kommen (page 177)
   Christus, der ist mein Leben (page 177)
   O Ewigkeit, du Donnerwort (page 179)
   Straf mich nicht in deinem Zorn (page 182)
   Jesu, du mein liebstes Leben (page 178)
   Werde munter, mein Gemüte (page 183)

H. Refer to Handel's "Hallelujah!" from the *Messiah* on page 207.

Examine measures 4–10. Identify any exceptions to standard voice-leading practice as stated in chapter 9. Describe any exceptions in the space below.

Review

The techniques of voice leading allow you to connect chords smoothly, creating parts that are easily singable. These techniques will not, in themselves, allow you to produce interesting music, but they are important standard procedures that you will use many times in future chapters, so it is important that they be thoroughly mastered.

1. Review the voice-leading principles for two-voice species counterpoint in chapter 8. Continue to write first-species counterpoints above and below each *cantus firmus* in the text and workbook. Most of the basic principles of voice leading in four voices come from species counterpoint.
2. Examine the soprano melodies of several of the Bach chorales on pages 177–183 in the anthology in relationship with the bass voices. Notice how the principles of species counterpoint are observed in these two-voice combinations.
3. Study the principles of four-voice writing on pages 162–166 and the common errors shown on pages 166–167. These guidelines will enable you to create smooth four-voice voice leading.
4. Since voice leading is a technique that can only be learned by practice, use figured basses that have not been assigned by your instructor for extra practice.

Test Yourself 9

Answers are on page 168.

1. Below is a four-voice chorale phrase that contains a number of errors in voice leading. Place Roman numerals in the blanks provided and describe the errors you see in the phrase.

1.   2.   3.   4.   5.   6. 7.   8.   9.   10. 11. 12. 13.   14.

2. Complete the second chord in each of the excerpts below. The key in each case is C major. Place Roman numerals in the blanks provided. Observe the figured bass symbols and pay particular attention to the chord qualities involved.

a.    b.    c.    d.

6

CM: __ __   __ __   __ __   __ __

e.    f.    g.    h.

6
4

6

CM: __ __   __ __   __ __   __ __

10 Harmonic Progression and Harmonic Rhythm

Name _____

Section _____

Date _____

A. Following are eight harmonized chorale phrases.
1. Analyze each chord using Roman numerals and indications for inversions.
2. Circle all nonharmonic tones and indicate the type by using the abbreviations in the following list.
3. Name the cadence type that concludes each phrase.

Nonharmonic Tones

PT = Unaccented passing tone
P̆T = Accented passing tone
NT = Neighboring tone
7–6 SUS = 7–6 suspension
4–3 SUS = 4–3 suspension
ET = Escape tone
A = Anticipation
APP = Appoggiatura

1.

(Key) ___: 1 2 3 4 5 6 7

Cadence _____

2.

(Key) ___: 1 2 3 4 5 6 7

Cadence _____

3.

(Key) ___: 1 2 3 4 5 6 7

Cadence _____

4.

(Key) ___: 1 2 3 4 5 6 7

Cadence _____

(Key)   1   2   3   4   5   6   7   (Key)   1   2   3   4   5   6   7

Cadence   Cadence

(Key)   1   2   3   4   5   6   7   (Key)   1   2   3   4   5   6   7

Cadence   Cadence

B. Following are three short excerpts in keyboard style.
   1. Bracket the harmonic rhythm.
   2. Analyze each harmonic area using Roman numerals and indications for inversions.
   3. Circle and identify any nonharmonic tones.
   4. Name the cadence type that concludes each phrase.

Pachelbel: Chaconne.

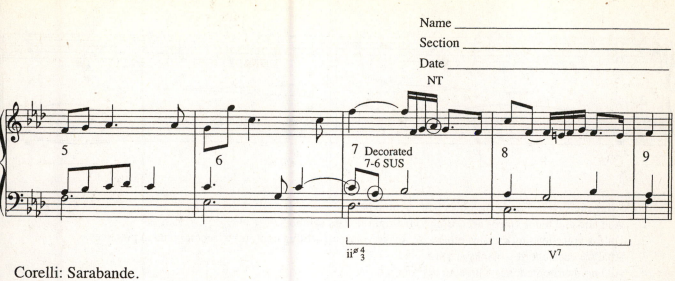

Corelli: Sarabande.

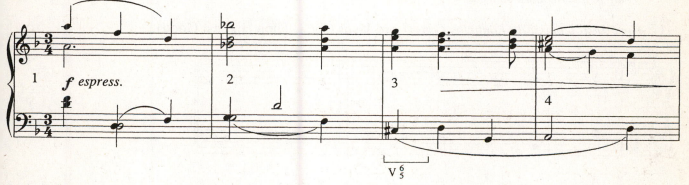

Brahms: Romance from Six Piano Pieces, op. 118, no. 5, m. 1–5.

C. Following are seven chorale melodies with figured bass.
  1. Add alto and tenor voices according to the figured bass symbols.
  2. Unless voice leading dictates otherwise, make your part writing conform to recommended practices.
  3. Analyze each chord—blanks are provided.
  4. Add nonharmonic tones wherever appropriate.
  5. Play your harmonization in class.

  1. *Herr Jesu Christ, du höchstes Gut* (Lord Jesus Chrst, Thou Highest Good).

_____ :   i   ___   ___   ___   ___   ___   ___
(Key)

  2. *Der Tag, der ist so Freudenreich* (This Day is so Joyful).

_____ :   I   ___   ___   ___   ___   ___
(Key)

  3. *Meinen Jesum lass ich nicht* (I Will Not Leave My Jesus).

_____ :   I   ___   ___   ___   ___   ___   ___
(Key)

Name _____

Section _____

Date _____

4. *Vom Himmel hoch da komm ich her* (From Heaven Above I Come).

_____ : ___vi___ _____ _____ _____
(Key)

5. *Du Friedensfürst, Herr Jesu Christ* (Thou Prince of Peace, Lord Jesus Christ).

_____ : ___I___ _____ _____ _____
(Key)

6. *Vater unser im Himmelreich* (Our Father Who Art in Heaven).

_____ : ___i___ _____ _____ _____
(Key)

7. *Wach auf, mein Herz, und singe* (Awake, My Heart, and Sing).

_____ : ___I___ _____ _____ _____
(Key)

D. Each exercise represents a figured bass voice.
   1. Complete the remaining three upper voices (soprano, alto, and tenor) according to the figuration supplied.
   2. Try to make each voice as interesting as possible, but the soprano should have priority. You will achieve maximum success by writing the entire soprano voice first, then filling in the alto and tenor as needed.
   3. Be sure to observe part-writing practices as cited in the text.
   4. Provide a complete Roman numeral analysis of each completed figured bass. Blanks are provided.

The Structural Elements of Music

5.

_____ :   i   __   __   __   __   __   __

(Key)

6.

_____ :   vi   __   __   __   __   __   __

(Key)

7.

_____ :   i   __   __   __   __   __

(Key)

E. Following are excerpts from six string quartets by Mozart.
   1. On a separate piece of paper, determine the harmonic rhythm—the number and placement of the triads.
   2. In a column under each change of harmony, write the letter names (designating the roots) or chord symbols for all possible triads that could be used to harmonize the melody.
   3. Indicate the obvious nonharmonic tones. These need not agree with the basic triads you select.
   4. Select the cadence chords.
   5. Draw a line between all adjacent chords whose roots form a descending P5th progression.
   6. Chart three or four possible harmonizations using a majority of ascending P4th progressions, separating such series with a descending 3rd or an ascending 2nd progression.
   7. Sing or play the melody and accompany it on the piano with each of your proposed harmonic selections.
   8. Experiment with different harmonic rhythms, using some containing frequent chord changes and others with very few.
   9. Play at least one of each student's harmonizations in class and have the class members determine which they find most appropriate.
   10. Arrange some of the harmonizations for string quartet, woodwind quartet, brass quartet, piano, harpsichord, or any other medium available to the class.

1. Mozart: String Quartet in G Major, K. 80, III (Trio), m. 1–8.

Tempo di Menuetto

2. Mozart: String Quartet in G Major, K. 80, IV (Rondeau), m. 1–8.

3. Mozart: String Quartet in G Major, K. 156, III (Tempo di Menuetto), m. 1–8.

4. Mozart: String Quartet in B-flat Major, K. 159, III (Rondo), m. 1–8.

Allegro grazioso

5. Mozart: String Quartet in C Major, K. 157, III.

Presto

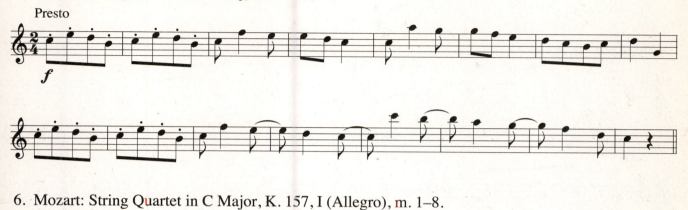

6. Mozart: String Quartet in C Major, K. 157, I (Allegro), m. 1–8.

F. Refer to the third movement of Mozart's String Quartet in G Major, K. 80, on page 232.
    1. Determine the harmonic rhythm.
    2. Provide a harmonic analysis below each chord.
    3. Circle all nonharmonic tones.
    4. Prepare a chart indicating the number of:
        a. Descending 5th (ascending 4th) progressions.
        b. Ascending 5th (descending 4th) progressions.
        c. Ascending 2nd (descending 7th) progressions.
        d. Descending 3rd (ascending 6th) progressions.
        e. Ascending 3rd (descending 6th) progressions.
        f. Descending 2nd (ascending 7th) progressions.

G. Refer to *Freu dich sehr, o meine Seele* from Album for the Young, op. 68, by Robert Schumann on page 239. Follow the same procedures as described in section B.

H. Following are several folk songs.
    1. First, determine the harmonic rhythm—the number and placement of the triads—for each.
    2. In a column under each change of harmony, write the letter names (designating the roots) or chord symbols for all possible triads that could be used to harmonize the melody.
    3. Indicate the obvious nonharmonic tones. These need not agree with the basic triads you select.
    4. Select the cadence chords.
    5. Draw a line between all adjacent chords whose roots form a descending P5th (ascending P4th) progression.
    6. Chart three or four possible harmonizations, using a majority of descending P5th progressions while separating such series with descending 3rd or ascending 2nd progressions.

7. Sing or play the melody and accompany it on the piano with each of your proposed harmonic selections.
8. Experiment with different harmonic rhythms, using some containing frequent chord changes and some with very few.
9. Play at least one of each student's harmonizations in class and have the class members determine which they find most appropriate.
10. Arrange some of the harmonizations for guitar, piano, instrumental ensembles, or any other medium available to the class.

1. Welsh Folk Song: "Ash Grove."

2. Irish Folk Song: "Cockles and Mussels."

3. Scottish Folk Song: "The Wearing of the Green."

The Structural Elements of Music

4. German Song: "Our Thoughts, They Are Free."

5. French Song: *"Au Clair de Lune."*

6. Minstrel Song: "Jimmy Crack Corn."

7. American Work Song: "I've Been Working on the Railroad."

Review

The technique of melody harmonization is at the heart of this chapter. The central importance of the circle of 5th progression (circle progression) in achieving a satisfactory harmonization cannot be overemphasized.

1. Choose a few pieces from a collection of traditional and patriotic songs, a hymnal, or some similar music. Name the root of each chord. (You may not be able to do a Roman numeral analysis of the entire piece because the chord vocabulary may not have been covered yet.) Mark each example of a circle progression you discover. Try to find examples of several circle progressions in succession. How often do these progressions reach the tonic chord as a target?
2. Review the sections on the vii° and the second inversion tonic triad on page 182 of the text. Remember that the leading-tone triad is closely related to the dominant and counts as a weaker circle progression when it progresses to the tonic chord. The tonic triad in second inversion is usually a decoration of the dominant chord that follows immediately.
3. Practice harmonizing chorale melodies, using examples from the assignments or familiar hymn tunes. Try to use as many circle progressions as possible in your harmonizations. Remember that each phrase must end with one of the standard cadences.
4. This would be a good time to review the materials of Chapters 5 and 9; you will need to have them clearly in mind as you work on your chorale harmonizations. Music theory is a cumulative subject, and you must constantly review previous materials to keep them fresh in your mind.

Test Yourself 10

Answers are on page 169.

Below are several phrases from a chorale setting by Otto Nicolai (1810–49) with each pair of chords identified by a number.

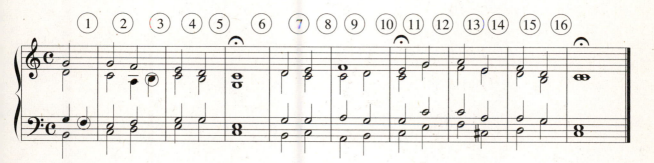

1. List all the progressions according to type, as follows:
    a. Circle progressions
    b. Descending 3rd progressions
    c. Ascending 2nd progressions
    d. Other progressions
2. What conclusion could you reach by studying the tabulation of progression types in question 1?
3. Below is a chorale melody with possible chords for a harmonization (only one choice is given for the first note of the melody and the final note of each phrase). Mark all possible circle progressions with a line between the Roman numerals. Choose a single chord for each quarter note that takes advantage of the maximum number of circle progressions. If no circle progression is possible try to choose an ascending 2nd or descending 3rd progression. You should have at least twelve circle progressions in your harmonization.
4. Compare your chord choices with the setting of this chorale by Bach on page 179. (Bach's setting uses 7th chords and some chromatic harmony that you have not studied as yet.) How often does your chord choice agree with that of Bach?

O Ewigkeit, du Donnerwort (Oh Eternity, Thou Word of Thunder).

The Dominant Seventh Chord

Name _____

Section _____

Date _____

A. Write a major-minor 7th chord above each of the ten given tones. The example illustrates the correct procedure.

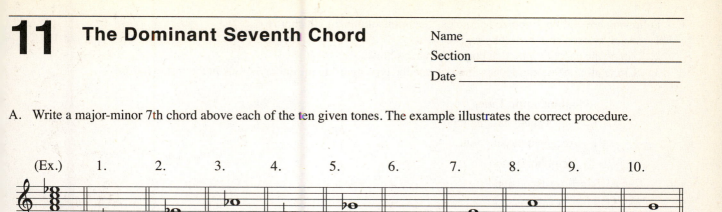

B. Each of the following chords is a dominant (major-minor) 7th.
1. Provide a circle resolution for each chord.
2. Analyze both chords—the chord succeeding the dominant 7th will be the tonic triad of a major key.
The example illustrates the correct procedure.

C. Following are eight harmonized chorales containing dominant 7th chords.
1. Analyze each chord. Blanks are provided.
2. Name the cadence type that concludes each phrase.
3. Circle all nonharmonic tones and indicate the type by using the abbreviations in the following list.

Nonharmonic Tones

PT = Unaccented passing tone
$\overset{>}{\text{PT}}$ = Accented passing tone
NT = Neighboring tone
7–6 SUS = 7–6 suspension
4–3 SUS = 4–3 suspension
ET = Escape tone
A = Anticipation
APP = Appoggiatura

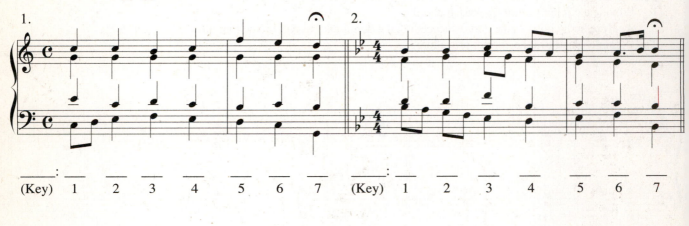

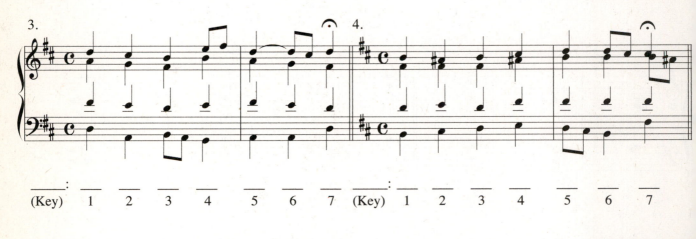

5.

(Key) ____ : ___ 1 ___ 2 ___ 3 ___ 4 ___ 5 ___ 6 ___ 7

Cadence _____

6.

(Key) ____ : ___ 1 ___ 2 ___ 3 ___ 4 ___ 5 ___ 6 ___ 7

Cadence _____

7.

(Key) ____ : ___ 1 ___ 2 ___ 3 ___ 4 ___ 5 ___ 6 ___ 7

Cadence _____

8.

(Key) ____ : ___ 1 ___ 2 ___ 3 ___ 4 ___ 5 ___ 6 ___ 7

Cadence _____

D. Following are seven chorale melodies with figured bass.
1. Add alto and tenor voices according to the figured bass symbols.
2. Make sure your part writing conforms to recommended practice.
3. Analyze each chord—blanks are provided.
4. Add chord tones and nonharmonic tones (usually eighth notes) to improve voice leading.
5. Play your harmonization in class.

1. *Schmücke dich o liebe Seele* (Prepare Thyself, Dear Soul).

____ : ___ I ___ ___ ___ ___ ___ ___ ___

(Key)

2. *Wenn wir in höchsten Nöten sein* (When We Are in Utmost Need).

_____ :   I   ___ ___ ___ ___ ___
(Key)

3. *Jesu, Jesu, du bist mein* (Jesus, Jesus, Thou Art Mine).

_____ :   I   ___ ___ ___ ___
(Key)

4. *Keinen hat Gott verlassen* (God Has Forsaken No One).

_____ :   ___ ___ ___ ___
(Key)

5. *Ich freue mich in dir* (I Rejoice in Thee).

_____ :   V   ___ ___ ___ ___ ___
(Key)

6. *Erwurgtes Lamm* (Slaughtered Lamb).

_____ :   vi   ___ ___ ___ ___ ___ ___ ___ ___
(Key)

7. *Mein Jesu, dem die Seraphim* (My Jesus, Whom the Seraphim).

_____ :   iii   ___ ___ ___ ___ ___ ___ ___
(Key)

E. Each exercise represents a figured bass voice.
1. Complete the remaining three upper voices (soprano, alto, and tenor) according to the figuration supplied.
2. Try to make each voice as interesting as possible, but the soprano should have priority. You will have best results by writing the entire soprano voice first, then filling in the alto and tenor as needed.
3. Be sure to observe voice-leading practices as cited in the text.
4. Provide a complete Roman numeral analysis of each completed figured bass. Blanks are provided.

1.

_____ :   iii   ___ ___ ___ ___ ___ ___
(Key)

2.

_____ :   I   __   __   __   __   __
(Key)

3.

_____ :   I   __   __   __   __
(Key)

4.

_____ :   V⁶   __   __   __   __   __
(Key)

5.

_____ :   iii   __   __   __   __   __   __   __
(Key)

6.

___ : ___ I ___ ___ ___ ___ ___ ___
(Key)

7.

___ : ___ I⁶ ___ ___ ___ ___ ___ ___
(Key)

F. Each of the following melodies is a folk song.
  1. Play or sing each melody several times. Determine the harmonic rhythm and place a bracket above the melody tones that will be supported by each harmony.
  2. Rewrite the melody on a separate sheet of score paper and indicate all possible traits that can harmonize the tones within each bracketed harmonic area.
  3. Play or sing the melody over again several times, experimenting with various different selected harmonies. When the V triad is indicated, try substituting the V⁷ chord.
  4. Select the series of triads and V⁷ chords you like best, and write them on the score paper beneath the melody.
  5. Be sure that descending P5th progressions play a prominent role in each harmonization. Also, include at least one or two V⁷ chords in each arrangement.
  6. Select an accompaniment figure that can be used more or less intact throughout. The accompaniment figure should fit the medium (piano, stringed instruments, woodwind instruments, brass instruments, and so on).

Possible accompaniment chords for piano:

Block Chord   1.   2.   3.   4.   5.

  7. Fit the accompaniment figure to each successive chord and complete the composition.
  8. Assign the melody itself to a solo voice or instrument. If you wish, make up some words of your own for the folk song melody.
  9. Play some of the compositions in class. Have the students decide which harmonic rhythm and harmonization is most suitable for the particular melody.

1. American Folk Song (This particular folk song is based on a pentatonic scale.)

2. Russian Folk Song.

Except for the beginning of each phrase, the following composition can be harmonized using descending P5th (ascending P4th) progressions.

3. Balkan Folk Song.

4. Russian Folk Song.

5. American Folk Song.

G. Refer to Mozart's *Das Kinderspiel,* which follows.
1. Have a member of the class play the composition while the sopranos sing the upper voice and the basses and baritones sing the lowest voice.
2. Bracket the harmonic rhythm; that is, place a bracket over the tones that fall within each harmony.
3. Do a Roman numeral analysis of the excerpt.
4. On a separate sheet of paper, indicate the type of resolution for each major-minor 7th chord (circle progression, non-circle progression with resolution, or nonresolution of the 7th factor).
5. Arrange this excerpt for a group of instruments played by members of the class.

Mozart: *Das Kinderspiel* (The Children's Game), K. 598, m. 1–8.

Munter

H. Follow the same procedures described in G above for the Sonatina in F, op. 55, no. 4, by Kuhlau on page 223.

Review

1. Look at the circle of 5ths on page 35 of the text. Spell the dominant 7th chord in each major and minor key. Remember to use the harmonic form of the minor scales. Write the dominant 7th in four parts and resolve it to the tonic chord, making sure that the 7th resolves downward by step. Use the first example in figure 11.9 on page 204 of the text as a model for your progression. Play the progressions on the piano.
2. Repeat the procedure above, resolving the dominant 7th chord to VI or vi. Use the second example in figure 11.10 on page 204 as a model for this progression. Play this progression on the piano.
3. Remember that the list of terms at the beginning of each chapter forms a convenient list of important concepts you need to understand. See if you remember the important information about each of the listed terms. Pay particular attention to the specific figured bass symbols for the inversions of the 7th chords.
4. Work out assignments that were not completed during your study of the chapter for practice in dealing with the dominant 7th chord.
5. Dominant 7th chords are by far the most common 7th chords in tonal music. Find examples of dominant 7ths in familiar music and see if the part-writing principles contained in this chapter are observed. Does the 7th of the chord move downward by step? If not, can you see how its resolution is accounted for in the music?

Test Yourself 11

Answers are on page 169.

Question 1 refers to this musical example:

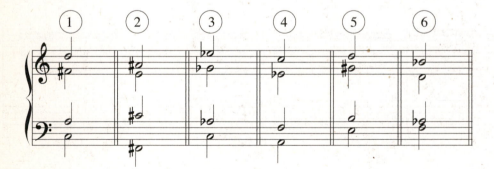

1. Each of the chords is a dominant 7th chord. Determine the chord and its inversion and answer the following questions.

   a. Chord number **1** is the dominant 7th chord in _____ major. The 7th is in the _____ voice and will resolve to _____ (note name) in the tonic triad.

   b. Chord number **2** is the dominant 7th chord in _____ minor. The 7th is in the _____ voice and will resolve to _____ (note name) in the tonic triad.

   c. Chord number **3** is the dominant 7th chord in _____ major. The 7th is in the _____ voice and will resolve to _____ (note name) in the tonic triad.

   d. Chord number **4** is the dominant 7th chord in _____ minor. The 7th is in the _____ voice and will resolve to _____ (note name) in the tonic triad.

   e. Chord number **5** is the dominant 7th chord in _____ minor. The 7th is in the _____ voice and will resolve to _____ (note name) in the tonic triad.

   f. Chord number **6** is the dominant 7th chord in _____ major. The 7th is in the _____ voice and will resolve to _____ (note name) in the tonic triad.

Questions 2–5 refer to the musical examples below:

2. Dominant 7th chords appear at chord numbers _____ , _____ , _____ , and _____ .

3. At chord number _____ the 7th of the dominant does not resolve in the normal manner.

4. Nonharmonic tone review:

   a. The nonharmonic tone at chord number **1** is a(n) _____ .

   b. The nonharmonic tone at chord number **3** is a(n) _____ .

   c. The nonharmonic tone at chord number **5** is a(n) _____ .

   d. The nonharmonic tone at chord number **6** is a(n) _____ .

   e. The nonharmonic tone at chord number **7** is a(n) _____ .

   f. The nonharmonic tone at chord number **10** is a(n) _____ .

   g. The nonharmonic tone at chord number **11** is a(n) _____ .

5. Cadence review:

   a. The cadence at chord number **4** is a(n) _____ cadence.

   b. The cadence at chord number **8** is a(n) _____ cadence.

   c. The cadence at chord number **12** is a(n) _____ cadence.

12 The Leading-Tone Seventh Chords

Name _____

Section _____

Date _____

A. Write the vii°⁷ chord above each root. The illustration demonstrates the correct procedure.

1. (Ex.) 2. 3. 4. 5. 6. 7. 8. 9. 10.

B. Write a vii⁰⁷ chord above each root. The illustration demonstrates the correct procedure.

11. (Ex.) 12. 13. 14. 15. 16. 17. 18. 19. 20.

C. Each four-voice chord below is either a vii°⁷ or vii⁰⁷ chord.
   1. Resolve each vii°⁷ chord to a minor triad.
   2. Resolve each vii⁰⁷ chord to a major triad.
   The resolution chord will always be the tonic triad and may be either in root position or in inversion. The illustration demonstrates correct procedure.

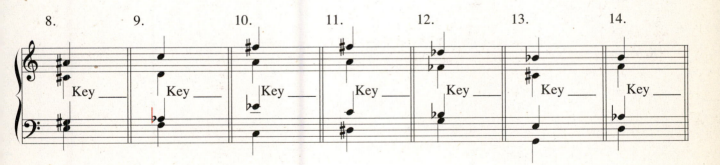

D. Each four-voice chord below is either a vii°⁷ or vii°⁷ chord. Resolve each leading-tone 7th chord to the V⁷ (or inversion) before continuing to the tonic. The illustration demonstrates the correct procedure.

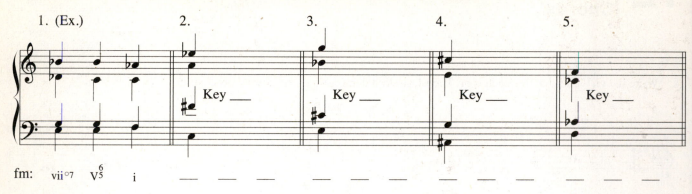

1. (Ex.)   2.   3.   4.   5.

Key ___   Key ___   Key ___   Key ___

fm: vii°⁷   V⁶₅   i   ___ ___ ___   ___ ___ ___   ___ ___ ___   ___ ___ ___

E. Each exercise below is a chorale melody with figured bass. All have been harmonized at least once by Bach.
   1. Add the alto and tenor voices according to the directions provided by the figured bass symbols.
   2. A slash (e.g., ⁴⁄₃) means to raise that interval (above the bass note) one half step.
   3. Double numbers (e.g., ⁸₈, ⁶₆, ³₃) mean to double that interval above the bass note.
   4. Analyze each chord using Roman numeral analysis.
   5. Sing or play each completed harmonization in class.

1. *Das alte Jahr vergangen ist* (The Old Year Has Passed Away).

___ : V⁶   ___   ___   ___   ___   ___   ___
(Key)

2. *Ach Gott, vom Himmel sieh darein* (Oh God, from Heaven Look Therein).

___ : V   ___   ___   ___   ___   ___   ___   ___
(Key)

3. *Herzlich tut mich verlangen* (I Desire Sincerely).

_____ :   ii°⁶   _____ _____ _____ _____ _____
(Key)

4. *Wir Christenleut* (We Christian People).

_____ :   V⁶   _____ _____ _____ _____ _____ _____
(Key)

5. *Jesu meine Freude* (Jesus, My Joy).

_____ :   i⁶   _____ _____ _____ _____ _____ _____
(Key)

F. The following are additional exercises related to the exercises in E.
    1. When completed, add at least four or five nonharmonic tones to each exercise.
    2. Play or sing these harmonizations in class and ask class members to determine which combinations sound most appropriate.

1.

_____: __ __ __ __ __
(Key)

2.

_____: __ __ __ __ __ __ __
(Key)

3.

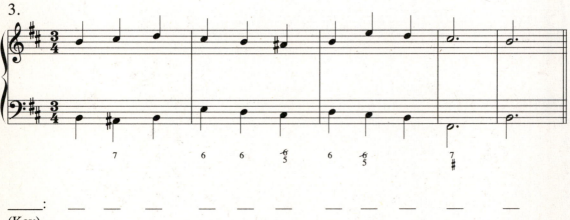

_____: __ __ __ __ __ __ __
(Key)

4.

_____ : __ __ __ __ __ __ __ __ __ __ __ __

(Key)

G. Each exercise represents a figured bass voice.
1. Complete the remaining upper voices (soprano, alto, and tenor) according to the figuration supplied.
2. Try to make each voice as interesting as possible, but the soprano should have priority. You will have most success by writing the entire soprano voice first, then filling in the alto and tenor as needed.
3. Be sure to observe part-writing practices as cited in the text.
4. Provide a complete Roman numeral analysis of each completed figured bass. Blanks are provided.

1.

_____ : __ __ i __ __ __ __ __ __ __ __

(Key)

2.

_____ : i⁶ __ __ __ vii°⁶ __ __ __ __ __ __

(Key)

3.

_____ : $\underline{\text{I}}$ ___ ___ ___ ___ ___ ___
(Key)

4.

_____ : $\underline{\text{i}}$ ___ ___ ___ ___ ___ ___
(Key)

5.

_____ : $\underline{\text{i}}$ ___ ___ ___ ___ ___
(Key)

6.

_____ : $\underline{\text{VI}}$ ___ ___ ___ ___ ___ ___
(Key)

The Structural Elements of Music

7.

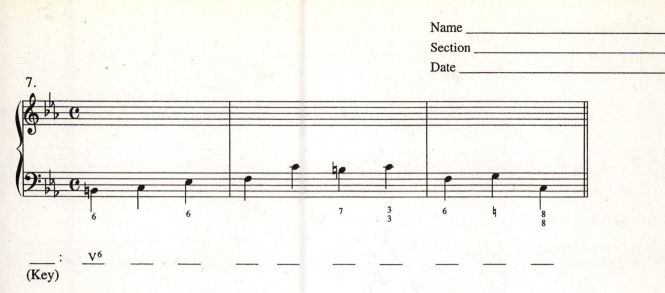

_____ :   V^6 ___   ___   ___   ___   ___   ___   ___

(Key)

H. Each of the following melodies is a folk song.

1. Play or sing each melody several times. Determine the harmonic rhythm and place a bracket above the melody tones that will be supported by each harmony.

2. Rewrite the melody on a separate sheet of score paper and indicate all possible triads that can harmonize the tones within each bracketed area.

3. Play or sing the melody again several times, experimenting with various harmonies. Indicate especially the points where a vii$^{\o7}$ or vii$^{\circ7}$ might occur.

4. Select the series of triads, dominant 7th chords, and leading-tone 7th chords you like best, and write them on the score paper beneath the melody.

5. Be sure that descending P5th (ascending P4th) progressions play a prominent role in each harmonization. Do not hesitate to exchange the vii$^{\o7}$ or vii$^{\circ7}$ for the V^7 where possible.

6. Select an accompaniment figure that can be used more or less intact throughout. The accompaniment figure should fit the medium (piano, stringed instruments, woodwind instruments, brass instruments, and so forth).

Possible accompaniment chords for piano:

7. Fit the accompaniment figure to each successive chord and complete the composition.

8. Assign the melody itself to a solo instrument. If you wish, write words of your own for the folk song melody.

9. Play some of the compositions in class. The students can decide which harmonic rhythm and harmonization is most suitable to the particular melody.

1. Russian Folk Song.

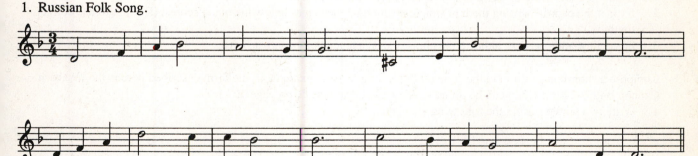

2. American Folk Song.

3. American Folk Song.

4. American Folk Song.

I. Refer to page 228 for an excerpt from the third movement of Mozart's Piano Sonata in A Minor, K. 310.
   1. Listen to a recording of this piece or to the excerpt played in class.
   2. Extract the chords, writing them in simple position on the staves below the piano scores. (Be sure to use correct rhythms.)
   3. For review and practice, indicate the phrases and cadence that punctuate each.

J. Compose a short composition in the style of a folk song. A good example of the form described here is the "Wabash Cannon Ball." (This melody can be found in chapter 13, exercise G, on page 127.)
   1. Write two phrases using the following elements:

Phrase	Number of Measures	Relationship	Cadence	Type
1	4	A	half	
2	4	AP	authentic	parallel

2. Use either a major or minor key. Include at least one vii⁰⁷ or vii°⁷ (leading-tone 7th chord). If you lack ideas, start with the following chords:

Measures:	1	2	3	4	5	6	7	8
Chords:	e	d♯°⁷	e	B⁷	e	a	B⁷	e

3. Compose the melody to fit the harmony.
4. Convert the block chords to an accompaniment pattern for either guitar or piano.
5. Compose words for the melody (if you wish).
6. Perform each student composition in class. Have one student sing the melody while another plays the accompaniment.

K. Refer to the introduction to the *Pathétique* Sonata for Piano, op. 13, by Beethoven on page 186.
1. Listen to a recording of this piece or to the excerpt played in class.
2. Do a roman numeral analysis of the excerpt.
3. Place an X above each major-minor, diminished-minor, and fully diminished 7th chord.

Review

1. Practice spelling leading-tone 7th chords in all major and minor keys. Remember that the leading-tone seventh in major is half-diminished while that in minor is fully diminished. How is the half-diminished 7th chord indicated in Roman numerals? The fully diminished 7th chord?
2. Play the examples in figure 12.13 (page 222 of the text) at the piano, observing the resolution of the 7th and the treatment of the tritones. Review the text associated with these examples.
3. Write the leading-tone 7th chord in a major or a minor key in four parts. Now resolve the chord to the tonic chord. The half-diminished 7th chord contains one perfect 5th (between the 3rd and 7th of the chord). Did you avoid parallel perfect 5ths in resolving this chord?
4. Look again at figure 12.13 on page 222 of the text. Play examples a and b at the piano. Now transpose these two examples to the keys of E-flat major and E-flat minor. Next move them to E major and E minor. Continue transposing these examples until you have played them in all keys.
5. Review the figured bass symbols for the inversions of 7th chords found on page 200 of the text (Chapter 11). Now complete several of the figured basses that were not assigned, paying particular attention to the resolution of the 7th and the tritones of the leading-tone 7th chords.

Test Yourself 12

Answers are on page 169.

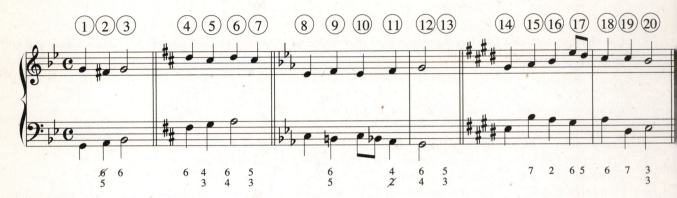

1. Place the twenty chords above in the following categories:

    a. Triad in root position _____

    b. Triad in first inversion _____

    c. Triad in second inversion _____

    d. V⁷ chord _____

    e. vii°⁷ chord _____

    f. viiø⁷ chord _____

FM: viiø⁷ I   em: vii°⁷ i⁶   AM: viiø⁶₅ I

2. Each of the examples above contains an error in the resolution of the leading-tone 7th chord. Describe the error in each case.

    a. _____

    b. _____

    c. _____

13 Nondominant Seventh Chords

Name _____

Section _____

Date _____

A. Write the requested 7th chord in simple position above the given tone.

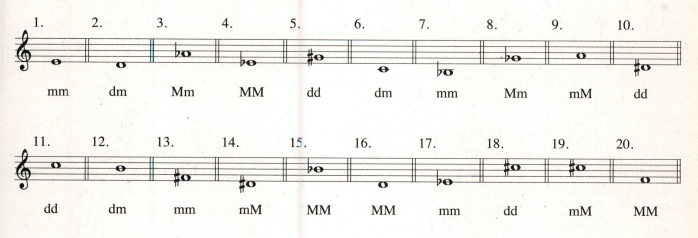

B. Provide the most common and often-used resolution for each of the 7th chords shown here. Analyze both chords in each exercise.

B♭M: ___ ___   AM: ___ ___   DM: ___ ___   EM: ___ ___   fm: ___ ___

CM: ___ ___   gm: ___ ___   DM: ___ ___   b♭m: ___ ___   BM: ___ ___

C. Give the chord analysis and the key (major and/or harmonic minor) in which the chord is diatonic.

1. (Ex.)

vii°⁷ in the key of E minor

2.

_____ in the key of _____

_____ in the key of _____

3.

_____ in the key of _____

_____ in the key of _____

_____ in the key of _____

4.

_____ in the key of _____

_____ in the key of _____

_____ in the key of _____

_____ in the key of _____

5.

_____ in the key of _____

D. Each exercise is a phrase of a chorale melody with bass and figured bass added. All were harmonized at least once by Bach.
1. Add alto and tenor as required by the figured bass. Remember that figured bass numbers indicate intervals above the bass note.
2. Eighth notes in circles (as in no. 4) are not to be harmonized.
3. Chord no. 5 in chorale 4 contains a 7th that is delayed in resolution. The resolution occurs in the second chord following the 7th chord.
4. Chords requiring other than first-choice doubling are indicated by special figured bass.
5. Analyze each chord—blanks are provided.
6. Arrange the chorale phrases for a quartet of instruments played by class members. Perform some of the harmonizations in class.

1. *Sei gegrüsset, Jesu gütig* (Hail to Thee, Jesus Kind).

6   4   6   7   7
         2

B♭M: vi ___ ___ ___ ___ ___ ___ ___ ___ ___

2. *Wach auf, mein Herz* (Awake, My Heart).

4   6   6   7
2   5

B♭M: I ___ ___ ___ ___ ___ ___ ___ ___

3. *Du, o schönes Weltgebäude* (Thou, O Fair Universe).

4   4   6   8   6   6
2   2   3   5   5

B♭M: vi ___ ___ ___ ___ ___ ___ ___ ___

4. *O wie selig seid ihr doch* (O How Blessed Ye Are).

3   7   8   7   6   6
3   6   5
            3

FM: vi ___ ___ ___ ___ ___ ___ ___ ___

5.

AM: I   __   __   __   __   __

6.

gm: i   __   __   __   __   __

E. Each exercise represents a figured bass voice.
1. Complete the remaining three upper voices (soprano, alto, and tenor) according to the figuration supplied.
2. Try to make each voice as interesting as possible, but the soprano should have priority. You will have the most success by writing the entire soprano voice first, then filling in the alto and tenor as needed.
3. Be sure to observe voice-leading practices as cited in the text.
4. Provide a complete Roman numeral analysis of each completed figured bass. Blanks are provided.

1.

GM: I   __   __   __   __   __   __

2.

A♭M: vi ___ ___ ___ ___

3.

am: i⁶ ___ ___ ___ ___ ___ ___ ___

4.

em: i ___ ___ ___ ___ ___ ___

5.

GM: I   ___ ___ . ___   ___ ___ ___

F.   Make a complete analysis of each of the following excerpts.
  1.   Provide a complete Roman numeral analysis.
  2.   On the score itself, circle those tones you consider to be nonharmonic.

1. Bach: *Jesu, meine Freude* (motet), BWV 227.

2. Mozart: Sonata in B-flat Major, K. 333, III, m. 68–71.

3. Mozart: Sonata in D Major, K. 284, Theme with Variations, Variation V, m. 14–17.

4. Debussy: *Claire de Lune* from *Suite Bergamasque*, m. 1–12.

pp   con sordino

vii°$\frac{4}{2}$/vi

V$\frac{6}{5}$/vi

5. Brahms: Ballade from Six Piano Pieces, op. 118, no. 3, m. 1–12.

gm: V^7 V^7/VII   V^7/iv   V^7/III

fm: E♭M:

G. Each of the following melodies is a folk song.
   1. Using the procedures outlined in Chapter 10 on harmonic progressions, harmonize each of the folk songs below.
   2. Experiment by trying a fast, medium, and slow harmonic rhythm. Then select the one you prefer for each melody.
   3. Write the accompaniment for guitar if the class has a guitar player. Have this student discuss writing accompaniments for the instrument. Range of the instrument, musical figures that lie easily under the fingers, and typical technical problems experienced by guitarists should be mentioned. (If the class has no guitar-playing member, write for a piano or instrumental combo.)
   4. Write words of your own to each melody.
   5. From the block chords of your original harmonization, fashion an accompaniment that fits the medium you choose.
   6. Perform the compositions in class. Have a voice student sing the melodies.

1. Russian Folk Song.

2. Folk Song: "The Wabash Cannonball."

Try to use one nondominant 7th chord in the harmonization of this melody.

In the following folk song, try a harmonization made up *entirely* of 7th chords.

3. Folk Song: "Shady Grove."

H. Refer to Bach's *Jesu, du mein liebstes Leben* on page 178.
   1. Analyze each chord.
   2. Indicate the resolution of each nondominant 7th chord type: 1, 2, or 3.
   3. Discuss modulations. Indicate whether they are common chord, chromatic, or phrase.
   4. Discuss the form of this composition.
   5. Enumerate the harmonic vocabulary used in this work.
   6. Divide the class into four sections (S,A,T,B) and sing the chorale. (Have a conducting major conduct the performance.)
   7. Arrange the composition for four instruments to be played by members of the class.

Review

1. Study the chart of diatonic 7th chords in figure 13.1 (pages 229–230 of the text). While this chart appears quite complicated, observe that there is considerable duplication among the various scales. For example, the supertonic 7th chord is a minor 7th chord in major and the ascending minor scales. It is a half-diminished 7th chord in the natural and harmonic forms of the minor. Learn the roman numeral symbols for each of the nondominant 7th chords.
2. Most nondominant 7th chords progress in a circle pattern. What chord will usually follow the supertonic 7th chord? The mediant 7th chord? The subdominant 7th chord? The submediant 7th chord? The tonic 7th chord?
3. Play the examples of nondominant 7th chord progressions in figures 13.7 and 13.8 (page 233 of the text), observing the common pattern in the circle progressions involving the nondominant 7th chords in root position (figure 13.7).
4. Write a mediant 7th chord in a major key in four parts. Resolve it in a circle progression to the submediant 7th chord. Continue the progression by resolving each 7th chord to another 7th chord in the circle pattern. Play the resulting progression at the piano. Repeat this pattern in minor, choosing the chords from the various forms of the scale that sound best to your ear.
5. Study the section on noncircle treatment of nondominant 7th chords on page 233 of the text. Do you observe any common pattern among these noncircle resolutions? Play the examples that illustrate each of these progressions (figure 13.7).

Test Yourself 13

Answers are on page 170.

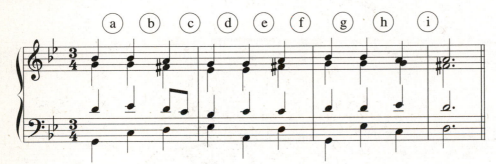

1. The chorale setting above contains a number of part-writing errors. Check each progression and describe any errors. There may be no errors, one error, or more than one error in any progression.

   a. _____
   b. _____
   c. _____
   d. _____
   e. _____
   f. _____
   g. _____
   h. _____
   i. _____

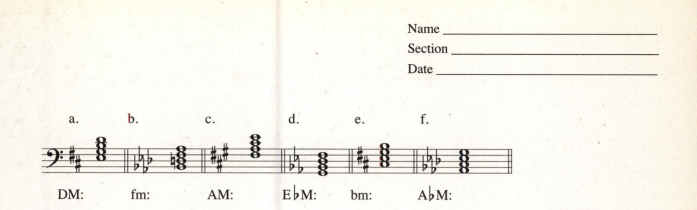

DM: fm: AM: E♭M: bm: A♭M:

2. Each chord above is a nondominant 7th chord in the given key. Give the proper Roman numeral for the chord. If the chord is resolved in a circle progression, what chord would follow?

a.   Roman numeral: _____ Roman numeral of following chord: _____

b.   Roman numeral: _____ Roman numeral of following chord: _____

c.   Roman numeral: _____ Roman numeral of following chord: _____

d.   Roman numeral: _____ Roman numeral of following chord: _____

e.   Roman numeral: _____ Roman numeral of following chord: _____

f.   Roman numeral: _____ Roman numeral of following chord: _____

14 Modulation

Name _____

Section _____

Date _____

A. Each exercise is a chorale melody with figured bass. All have been harmonized at least once by Bach.
1. Add the alto and tenor voices according to the directions provided by the figured bass symbols.
2. Make sure your part writing conforms to recommended practice.
3. Analyze each chord and indicate the point of modulation with a bracket similar to the model shown here:

CM: I   ii⁶   V   ⎡I
                                  GM: ⎣IV   ii⁶   V   I

4. Blanks are omitted to allow for proper bracketing.
5. Occasional overlapping of voices may be necessary between phrases, as in numbers 6–10.
6. Sing or play your completed harmonization in class.

1. *Ermuntre dich, mein schwacher Geist* (Rouse Thyself, My Weak Spirit).

FM: I

2. *O Jesulein süss, o Jesulein mild* (O Sweet Child Jesus, O Gentle Child Jesus).

gm: III

3. *Gott hat das Evangelium* (God Gave the Gospel).

em: i

4. *Meines Lebens letzte Zeit* (The Last Hour of My Life).

em: i

5. *Jesu, deine Liebes wunden* (Jesus, Thy Dear Wounds).

am: i

B. The following are additional exercises related to the exercises in A.
1. When completed, add at least four or five nonharmonic tones to each exercise.
2. Play these harmonizations in class and ask class members to determine which combinations sound most appropriate.

1.

2.

3.

4.

5.

Modulation 133

C. Each exercise represents a figured bass voice.
   1. Complete the remaining three upper voices (soprano, alto, and tenor) according to the figuration supplied.
   2. Try to make each voice as interesting as possible, but the soprano should have priority. You will have maximum success by writing the entire soprano voice first, then filling in the alto and tenor as needed.
   3. Be sure to observe part-writing practices as cited in the text.
   4. Provide a complete Roman numeral analysis of each completed figured bass. Blanks are omitted to allow for proper bracketing.

1.

bm: i

2.

am: i

3.

CM: I

4.

em: V

5.

DM: I

6.

gm: i

7.

B♭M: V⁶

D. Make a complete analysis of the Andante Cantabile, the second movement of the Sonatina, op. 88, no. 2, by Kuhlau (see page 224). Also include an analysis of phrases, periods. and nonharmonic tones.

E. Write a short composition of two phrases (eight measures).
1. Write out the following chord progressions in block harmony (chords in simple position).

| *Phrase 1:* | fm: | i | vii$^{\circ 7}$ | i | i^6 | i$^6_4$ | V |
| *Phrase 2:* | fm: | i | vii$^{\circ 7}$ | i | i^6 | | |

Phrase 2 continues: cm: [i   V^7 i] with v above

2. Each phrase should be four measures long in $\frac{6}{8}$ meter.
3. The two phrases should be parallel (measures 5 and 6 the same or nearly the same as 1 and 2).
4. Distribute the block chords in each phrase to produce musical balance.
5. Above the chords, write a melody using essentially eighth-note movement.
6. Write the composition for piano, solo instrument and piano, or for any combination of instruments played by class members.
7. From the block chords, fashion an accompaniment to the melody. Make sure the accompaniment is appropriate for the medium chosen.
8. Play the composition in class. If the composition is for a group of instruments, have a conducting student direct it.

F. Write an original composition.
1. Use the same harmonic vocabulary as found in the Andante Cantabile on page 224, including all chords studied to date.
2. Use the following form:

Phrase Number	Relationship	Key	Cadence
1	A	D major	Half cadence in D major
2	AP (parallel to A)	Modulate from D major to A major	Authentic cadence in A major
3	B (contrasting)	Begin in F♯ minor and modulate to D major	Half cadence in D major
4	A' (parallel to A)	D major throughout (do not modulate)	Authentic cadence in D major

3. Use homophonic texture (melody with chordal accompaniment).
4. Write for piano alone or for a solo instrument with piano accompaniment.
5. Although in writing for piano you may use a "broken" style (a style in which there is no set number of voices—you may range from three voices to five or six), use good part-writing procedures studied in four-voice chorale writing.
6. Suggested steps in completing the composition:
    a. First, prepare a set of chord progressions for each phrase—chords that will accommodate the modulations easily. At this point, the chords may be simply blocked out with no voice leading present. Proper selection of the basic chords is most important and gives direction to the composition.
    b. Next, write a melody to fit with the chord progressions.
    c. Now change the block chords into a pianistic arrangement that flows well. One possibility is to use Alberti bass (the arpeggiation of blocked chords).
    d. Finally, add expression, tempo, and phrase markings to provide a musical interpretation.

Remember that composing is the technique of manipulating and arranging musical tones. Development of the skills required to prepare a composition is very important in understanding music.

G. Following is the first phrase of the chorale melody, *O Haupt voll Blut und Wunden,* composed by Hans Leo Hassler (1564–1612) and appearing for the first time in the year 1601. This melody became quite popular and was harmonized by a variety of composers, including Johann Sebastian Bach.

Hassler: *O Haupt voll Blut und Wunden* (O Sacred Head Now Wounded).

1. Using the procedures outlined in Chapter 10 on harmonic progressions, harmonize this melody in four-part vocal style in the following four ways:
   a. First, harmonize the melody entirely in the key of C major.
   b. Next, harmonize the same melody entirely in the key of A minor.
   c. The third harmonization should begin in A minor and modulate to C major.
   d. The fourth harmonization should begin in C major and modulate to A minor.
2. If you can, play each harmonization on the piano in four-part harmony. If you are unable to do so, play each in its block-chord form (chords in simple position).
3. Determine which of the four you like best. Add appropriate nonharmonic tones to the four parts, distributing continuous eighth-note movement among the different voices.
4. Each class member should put his or her completed harmonizations on the blackboard or overhead projector. The entire class should then sing each one, conducted by a student.
5. Return now to the block-chord version of the harmonization. Devise an appropriate instrumental accompaniment pattern that can be applied more or less to each chord. The following illustrations may provide ideas:

Simple accompaniment, two voices:

More complex accompaniment, two voices:

Melody with accompaniment, two voices:

6. Complete the chorale prelude (the chorale melody with the instrumental accompaniment pattern) for piano, organ, or instrumental ensemble and perform it in class.

Review

1. Select a major or minor triad. List all major and minor keys in which that triad appears. (For example, the C-major triad appears in CM, FM, GM, am, fm, em). The triad can serve as a pivot chord in a common chord modulation between any two keys. Select two keys on the list and analyze the selected triad in both keys.

2. Turn to the Bach chorale settings in the anthology. Examine the beginning and end of each phrase to determine the key(s) at both points. If the key is different at the end of the phrase than at the beginning, complete a Roman numeral analysis to determine the point of modulation. Is the modulation a common chord or chromatic modulation? (If you are not sure of the difference, see figures 14.2 and 14.4 on pages 244–245 of the text, which illustrate each type.) Are there any examples of phrase modulation in the chorales? What is the difference between a phrase modulation and a common chord modulation?

3. The diminished 7th chords are favorite vehicles for enharmonic modulation, since they may be spelled in a variety of ways. Select a diminished 7th chord and write at least four enharmonic spellings. For each spelling determine the key in which it would be the leading-tone 7th chord. This chord can function as a pivot chord between any two of those keys.

Test Yourself 14

Answers are on page 170.

1. Write all possible diatonic pivot chords between the given keys:
    a. Example: B♭ major and F major

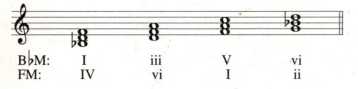

    B♭M: I   iii   V   vi
    FM: IV   vi   I   ii

    b. D major and G major
    c. F♯ natural minor and A major
    d. E natural minor and C major
    e. F natural minor and D♭ major
    f. B major and D♯ natural minor
    g. G♯ harmonic minor and B major
    h. G harmonic minor and D harmonic minor
    i. E major and F♯ natural minor

2. Provide a complete harmonic analysis for each chorale phrase. The example shows the proper way to analyze the pivot chord and subsequent modulation. Use the same procedure in your own analyses.

(Ex.)

CM: I   V^6 I   ⌈vi

am: ⌊i   V^7 i

a.

____ :

b.

____ :

c.

_____:

d.

_____:

Secondary Dominants and Leading-Tone Chords

Name _____

Section _____

Date _____

A. Write the five secondary dominant chord types for the chord that appears at the end of each of the scores. Note the example.

(Ex.)

GM: V/ii   V⁷/ii   vii°/ii   vii°⁷/ii   vii°⁷/ii   ii

1. E♭M: vi

2. c♯m: iv

3. fm: V

4. B♭M: iii

5. bm: V

6. AM: IV

7. em: VI

8. BM: ii

B. Complete each exercise in the following manner:
    1. Write the normal resolution for each secondary dominant or leading-tone 7th chord on the staff in four-part harmony.
    2. Analyze the resolution chord in the blank provided below the staves.
    3. Write the name of the key in the blank between the staves.
    Note the example.

(Ex.)   1.   2.   3.

CM: V⁷/IV   IV   ___: V⁶/ii   ___: vii°⁷/V   ___: V⁴₂/VI   (VI⁶)
              Resolution
              Chord

    4.   5.   6.   7.

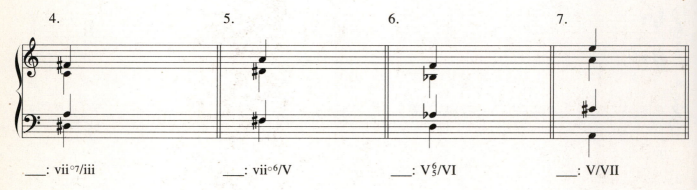

___: vii°⁷/iii   ___: vii°⁶/V   ___: V⁶₅/VI   ___: V/VII

    8.   9.   10.   11.

___: vii°⁷/V   ___: vii°⁶₅/IV   ___: vii°⁴₂/V   (V⁶₄)   ___: vii°⁷/vi

C. A secondary dominant or leading-tone chord is analyzed in different keys, depending on the function of the chord to which it progresses. Assume in all cases that the chord following provides the most common type of progression for that particular chord. Name the key of the chord using the analysis given. Note the example.

(Ex.)

vii°⁷/V in the key of <u>D major-minor</u>

vii°⁷/ii in the key of <u>G major</u>

vii°⁷/iv in the key of <u>e minor</u>

vii°⁷/VI in the key of <u>c# minor</u>

vii°⁷/iii in the key of <u>F major</u>

1.

V^6_5/V in the key of _____

V^6_5/ii in the key of _____

V^6_5/iv in the key of _____

V^6_5/vi in the key of _____

V^6_5/iii in the key of _____

2.

V⁶/ii in the key of _____

V⁶/VI in the key of _____

V⁶/iii in the key of _____

V⁶/V in the key of _____

V⁶/IV in the key of _____

3.

vii°⁷/iv in the key of _____

vii°⁷/iii in the key of _____

vii°⁷/V in the key of _____

vii°⁷/ii in the key of _____

vii°⁷/VI in the key of _____

D. Each exercise is a phrase of a chorale melody with bass and figured bass added. All were harmonized at least once by Bach.
1. Add alto and tenor as required by the figured bass.
2. Analyze each chord. Blanks are provided for all except chorale no. 3, which modulates.
3. Arrange the chorale phrases for a quartet of instruments played by class members. Perform some of the harmonizations in class.

1. *Herzlich lieb hab ich dich, o Herr*   (Dearly I Love Thee, O Lord).

E♭M: I   __   __   __   __   __   __   __

2. *Herr, wie du willst, so schicks mit mir*   (Lord, Ordain What Thou Wilt for Me).

CM: I   __   __   __   __   __   __   __

3. *Herzlich lieb hab ich dich, o Herr* (Dearly I Love Thee, O Lord).

cm: V

E. The following are additional chorale phrases. After completing the harmonizations, add at least four or five nonharmonic tones, including suspensions.

1.

2.

3.

4.

F. Each exercise represents a figured bass voice.
1. Complete the remaining three upper voices (soprano, alto, and tenor) according to the figuration supplied.
2. Try to make each voice as interesting as possible, but the soprano should have priority. You will have the most success by writing the entire soprano voice first, then filling in the alto and tenor as needed.
3. Be sure to observe voice-leading practices as cited in the text.
4. Provide a complete Roman numeral analysis of each completed figured bass. Blanks are provided, except for exercise no. 3, which modulates.

1.

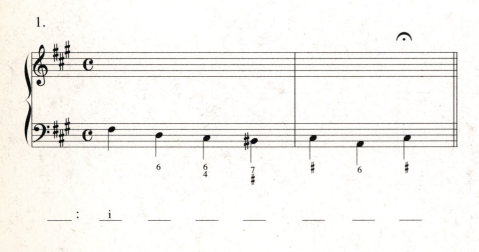

2.

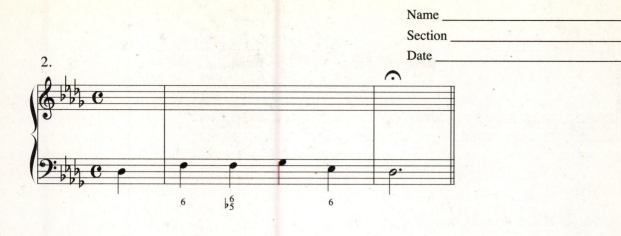

D♭M: I   ___   ___   ___

3.

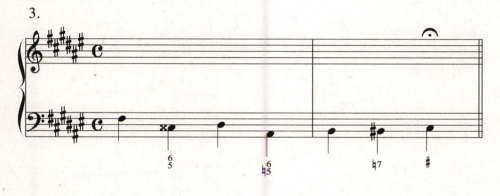

F♯M: I   ___   ___   ___   ___

4.

em: i   ___   ___   ___   ___   ___

5.

B♭M: I   ___   ___   ___   ___

6.

EM: I   ___ ___ ___ ___ ___

G. Do an analysis of each of the following excerpts from music literature.

1. Schumann: *Der arme Peter,* op. 53, no. 3, from *Romanzen und Balladen* (Langsam), m. 1–4.

2. Brahms: Waltzes, op. 39, no. 4, m. 1–10.

3. Schumann: *Novelletten,* op. 21, no. 8, *Fortsetzung und Schluss,* m. 282–291.

4. Joplin: "Weeping Willow," m. 13–20.

H. On a separate sheet of paper, write a period consisting of two 4-measure phrases.
   1. Use the following chord progressions:

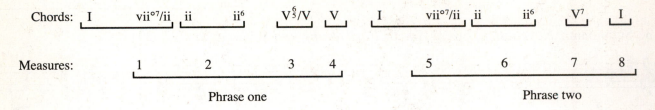

Chords: I · vii°⁷/ii · ii · ii⁶ · V⁶₅/V · V · I · vii°⁷/ii · ii · ii⁶ · V⁷ · I

Measures: 1 · 2 · 3 · 4 · 5 · 6 · 7 · 8

Phrase one · Phrase two

2. Use the key of E-flat major and $\frac{6}{8}$ meter.
3. Write in homophonic style (melody with chordal accompaniment).
4. Make the two phrases parallel (measures 1 and 2 similar to 5 and 6, while 3 and 4 contrast with 7 and 8).
5. Include at least one sequence.
6. Compose your own theme (melody) or employ the following motive:

I. All accidentals have been deleted from this excerpt from Mozart's Symphony in G Minor. Add accidentals to create secondary dominant or leading-tone chords. Then check the score in your library to see what secondary dominants Mozart intended. Analyze your finished product.

Mozart: Symphony in G Minor, K. 550, IV (Allegro assai), m. 1–8.

J. Write a composition according to the following guidelines:
1. Sixteen measures in length.

2. In $\frac{6}{8}$ meter.

3. In harmonic rhythm of one chord per measure (two chords per measure can be used in measures near the cadence).
4. In four phrases, with the following relationship:

Phrase	Type	Key	Cadence
1	A	G minor	Half cadence in G minor
2	B (contrast)	G minor modulating to D minor	Authentic cadence in D minor
3	A'	G minor	Half cadence in G minor
4	C	G minor	Authentic cadence in G minor

5. For piano or an instrument with piano accompaniment.
6. Using at least three secondary dominant or leading-tone chords.

K. Refer to the excerpt from the fourth movement of Ludwig van Beethoven's (1770–1827) String Quartet in C Minor, op. 18, no. 4 (composed around 1799) on page 191.
1. Copy the harmony (only) of the string quartet score on the piano staves provided. Be sure to copy every harmony tone from the score in the same octave—keep the texture the same as it appears in the score.
2. Analyze the harmony.
3. Discuss the use of:
   a. Secondary dominants
      i. Type 1, type 2, or type 3
      ii. Relationship to modulation
   b. Sequences
      i. Melodic sequences
      ii. Harmonic sequences (especially P5th descending chains)
   c. Key relationships and types of modulation
   d. Doubling and spacing in the chords

L. The following excerpt is from the famous Maple Leaf Rag, written in 1899 by Scott Joplin (1868–1917).
1. Listen as a member of the class plays the excerpt.
2. Extract the melody only (the highest-sounding tones) and write it on the staves above each piano score.
3. On a separate sheet of paper, analyze the melody for the following:
   a. The phrases (length, number, and relationship of one to another);
   b. Characteristics of the melody such as syncopation, outlining of triads, nonharmonic tones, and so on.
4. Write a complete harmonic analysis (Roman numeral analysis).
5. In class, play or sing the extracted melody along with the extracted chords in simple position. Then have a member of the class play the excerpt as it was written by Joplin. Discuss the ways in which Joplin adapted the melody and block chords to pianistic writing.
6. Discuss the style (melodic, harmonic, and rhythmic) in relation to other popular styles with which class members are familiar.
7. Have a member or members of the class transcribe the excerpt for a small combo and perform it in class.

M. Compose a short work of sixteen measures in the ragtime style for piano or for any combination of instruments played by class members. Use the excerpt from Maple Leaf Rag as a model for form and style.

N. Refer to Brahms's *Sehnsucht* on page 196 and Haydn's Sonata in E Minor on page 219.
1. Do a complete analysis of these two compositions.
2. Write a short paper of 200–500 words:
   a. Describing how circle progressions shape the harmonic flow of each composition.
   b. Comparing the Haydn and Brahms compositions. Contrast the use of circle progressions in each.
   c. Indicating key relationships in each. The key relationships in the Brahms work are more complicated. Explain why.
   d. Including information concerning the phrase relationships in both works.
   e. Indicating any other items you think are interesting.

Review

1. Select a major key and write all the diatonic major and minor triads in that key (I, ii, iii, IV, V, vi). Now spell the secondary dominant and secondary leading-tone chords for each of these triads. Take note of the accidentals required for each of these chords. Only those chords that have accidentals outside the original key signature are considered secondary dominants or leading-tone chords.
2. Any major-minor 7th chord can be a secondary dominant in a number of keys. Select a major-minor 7th chord; spell the major and the minor triad it would normally resolve to (in a circle progression). List all the major and minor keys that contain the major or minor triad above. Analyze the given major-minor 7th chord in each of those keys.

(Ex.)

Major-minor 7th chord:	G B D F (G7)
Resolves to:	C E G (C) or C E♭ G (c)
Keys containing C chord:	CM, GM, FM, am, fm, dm, em.
Keys containing cm chord:	B♭M, A♭M, E♭M, cm, gm.
Analyses of G^7 chord:	

CM: V^7	GM: V^7/IV	FM: V^7/V	am: V^7/III
fm: V^7/V	em: V^7/VI		
B♭M: V^7/ii	A♭M: V^7/iii	E♭M: V^7/vi	cm: V^7	gm: V^7/iv

3. Select a diminished 7th chord, spell the minor triad it would normally resolve to, then list the keys containing that minor triad. Analyze the given diminished 7th chord in each of those keys.

(Ex.)
Diminished 7th chord: B D F A♭ (b°7)
Resolves to: C E♭ G (c)
Keys containing c chord: B♭M, A♭M, E♭M, cm, gm
Analyses of b°7 chord:

B♭M: vii°7/ii   A♭M: vii°7/iii   E♭M: vii°7/vi   cm: vii°7
gm: vii°7/iv

Test Yourself 15

Answers are on page 172.

1. A secondary dominant or leading-tone chord is analyzed in different keys, depending on the function of the chord to which it progresses. Assume in all cases that the chord following the given chord is the most common resolution of that chord.

(Ex.)

a.

Name the key of the chord using the analysis given. Note the example.

vii°7/V in the key of <u>D major-minor</u>

vii°7/ii in the key of <u>G major</u>

vii°7/iv in the key of <u>e minor</u>

vii°7/VI in the key of <u>c♯ minor</u>

V^6_5/V in the key of _____

V^6_5/ii in the key of _____

V^6_5/iv in the key of _____

V^6_5/vi in the key of _____

b.

vii°7/iii in the key of <u>F major</u>

V^6/ii in the key of _____

V^6/VI in the key of _____

V^6/iii in the key of _____

V^6/V in the key of _____

V^6/IV in the key of _____

c.

V^6_5/iii in the key of _____

vii°7/iv in the key of _____

vii°7/iii in the key of _____

vii°7/V in the key of _____

vii°7/ii in the key of _____

vii°7/VI in the key of _____

2. Write the normal resolution for each secondary dominant or leading-tone 7th chord below in four-part harmony, being careful to properly resolve the active tones according to the voice-leading practices listed on pages 269 and 272 of the text. Name the key and provide a Roman numeral analysis of the resolution chord. Note the example.

(Ex.)   CM: V⁷/IV   IV Resolution Chord

a. ____: V⁶/ii

b. ____: vii°⁷/V

c. ____: V⁴₂/VI⁶

d. ____: vii°⁷/iii

e. ____: vii°⁶/V

f. ____: V⁶₅/VI

g. ____: V/VII

h. ____: vii°⁷/iv

i. ____: viiø⁶₅/ii

j. ____: vii°⁴₂/V

k. ____: vii°⁷/vi

16 Two-Part (Binary) Form

Name _____

Section _____

Date _____

A. For each of the following compositions:
1. Complete an analysis of the compositions.
2. Bracket each phrase.
3. Name the type of cadence at the end of each phrase.
4. Circle motives or themes that appear in both the A and B sections.
5. In your own words, indicate the relationship between the two sections.
6. Compare the form and construction of the compositions listed here.

   Bach: Sarabande from French Suite no. 1. (See page 180.)
   Corelli: Corrente. (See page 197.)
   Farnaby: The New Sa-Hoo (written circa 1595). (See page 203.)
   Handel: Sarabande from Harpsichord Suite no. 5. (See page 215.)
   Handel: Gigue from Harpsichord Suite no. 7. (See page 205.)
   Handel: Sarabande from Harpsichord Suite no. 4. (See page 213.)
   Haydn: Sonata in E Major, II, Hob. XVI: 13. (See page 219.)
   Haydn: Sonata in C Major, 35 Hob. XVI, III. (See page 222.)
   Kuhlau: Sonatina op. 55, no. 4, II. (See page 223.)
   Mozart: Sonata K. 331. (See page 231.)
   Schumann: *Kleine Romanze* (Little Romance) from Album for the Young, op. 68. (See page 240.)
   Schumann: *Davidsbündlertänze,* op. 6, no. 8. (See page 236.)

B. Write a composition using the following directions:

Measures	Key	Types of Cadence	Phrase Relationship	Remarks
Part A				
1–4	B-flat major	Half in B-flat	A	
5–8	B-flat major modulating to F major	Authentic— F major	AP	A parallel.
Part B				
9–12	F major	Half—F major	A'	Development of A motive or idea from phrase A.
13–16	F major modulating to B-flat major	Authentic in B-flat major	B	Different material.

C. Write a composition in two-part form.
1. There are no restrictions on the content of this composition whatsoever, except that it must be in two-part form.
2. The composition should be of at least sixteen measures.
3. Write the composition for any instrument, voice, or combination of the two.
4. Play the composition in class.

D. Analysis:
1. Have a member of the class who is a piano student play the *Thema* (theme) by Beethoven. (See page 195.)
2. Make a complete melodic, harmonic, and formal analysis of the excerpt.
3. Have one member of the class arrange the excerpt for three or four instruments (such as a bassoon and two clarinets).
4. Perform the arrangement in class.
5. Sing the entire composition as written, using a neutral syllable, such as *lo, la,* or *ta.*

E. Analysis:

Using the procedures listed in section D, make a complete melodic, harmonic, and formal analysis of the Largo by Arcangelo Corelli (1653–1713), found on page 199.

Review

Chapter 16 deals with larger areas of musical structure and will require a new approach to study. Previous chapters required fluency in spelling chords and knowledge of the specifics of voice leading, which can be practiced, whereas this chapter requires an understanding of larger concepts and can be reviewed in much the same way you would review the materials of other textbooks.

1. Play or listen to a recording of each of the compositions analyzed in this chapter. Carefully examine the analysis of each composition, including the analytical statements in the scores themselves and the summary analysis that follows. Make certain that you understand each analytical statement. If certain items are not clear to you, reread the pertinent section of the chapter or look in previous chapters for an explanation. If you still have problems, discuss them with your instructor or a fellow student.

2. Define each term listed at the head of the chapter (page 295 in the text) in your own words. Compare your definition with the definition of the glossary and see if you can improve your definition. Consider how the terms can be applied to the compositions in the chapter.

Test Yourself 16

Answers are on page 173.

1. Examine measures 1–8 of figure 16.4 on page 298 of the text. Would you describe the form of this section as open or closed? Why? What about the remaining section (measures 9–18)?

2. Examine measures 1–8 of figure 16.5 on pages 299–300 of the text. Would you describe the form of this section as open or closed? Why? What about the remaining section (measures 9–34)?

3. We have used the terms *phrase, period,* and *section* to designate the elements of form. Define each of these terms to make a clear distinction among them. Can a phrase ever be a period? Can a period ever be a section? Why or why not?

17 Three-Part (Ternary) Form

Name _____

Section _____

Date _____

A. Analysis:
1. Listen as a member of the class plays *Erinnerung* (Remembrance) from Album for the Young by Schumann. (See page 238.)
2. Provide a complete harmonic, melodic, and formal analysis of the excerpt.
3. Have one member of the class arrange the excerpt for three or four instruments (such as a bassoon and two clarinets).
4. Perform the arrangement in class.
5. Sing the entire composition as written (sing the notes on a neutral syllable, such as *lu, la,* or *ta*).

B. Analysis:

Employ the same procedures as in section A to devise an analysis of Beethoven's Sonata in E-flat, op. 31, no. 3, III. (Refer to page 187.)

C. Analysis:

Employ the same procedures as in section A to devise an analysis of Grieg's *Volkweise* (Folk Song), op. 38. (Refer to page 204.)

D. Analysis:

Employ the same procedures as in section A to devise an analysis of Schumann's *Wilder Reiter* (Wild Rider) from Album for the Young, op. 68. (Refer to page 242.)

E. Write a short composition in three-part form.
1. Pattern the form after *Wilder Reiter* (section D above) by Schumann.
2. The composition should be homophonic (a clearly defined melody with harmonic and rhythmic accompaniment).
3. Use *only* the harmonic vocabulary studied to date.
4. Utilize compositional procedures found in Chapter 10 of the textbook, "Harmonic Progression."
5. Write the composition for any instrument, voice, or combination thereof that class members can play.
6. When the composition is completed, each student should perform or have his or her work performed in class.
7. Each composition should be critiqued by class members.

Review

Chapter 17, like the previous chapter, deals with larger areas of musical structure. This chapter can be studied in much the same way as Chapter 16.

1. Play or listen to a recording of each of the compositions analyzed in this chapter. Carefully examine the analysis of each composition, including the analytical statements in the scores themselves and the summary analysis that follows. Make certain that you understand each analytical statement. If certain items are not clear to you, reread the pertinent section of the chapter or look in previous chapters for an explanation. If you still have problems, discuss them with your instructor or a fellow student.
2. Define each term listed at the head of the chapter (page 311 in the text) in your own words. Compare your definition with the definition of the glossary and see if you can improve your definition. Consider how the terms can be applied to the compositions in the chapter.

Test Yourself 17

Answers are on page 173.

1. Examine measures 1–16 of figure 17.2 on pages 312–313 of the textbook. Would you describe the form of this section as open or closed? Why?
2. Examine measures 17–32 of figure 17.2 on pages 313–314 of the text. Would you describe the form of this section as open or closed? Why?
3. Describe the function of the B section of a three-part (ternary) form.
4. In this chapter a form called rounded binary form was discussed. How does the rounded binary form differ from a three-part (ternary) form?
5. A ternary form may be expanded in two ways: by repetition of a section or by the appearance of auxiliary formal members. Name three auxiliary members that may be added to the basic three-part design.

Answers to Self-Tests

Test Yourself 1 (page 6)

1. (Answers in parentheses are the alternate system of octave identification shown in figure 1.9.)
   a. e^l (E^4)   b. d^2 (D^5)   c. B (B^2)   d. E (E^2)   e. f^1 (F^4)   f. f (F^3)
   g. e (E^3)   h. g^1 (G^4)   i. c^3 (C^6)   j. g (G^3)   k. AA (A^1)   l. f^1 (F^4)
2. Pairs: (a–i)   (b–d)   (c–h)   (e–g)   (f–j)
3. a. Forte should not be on the staff.
   b. 1. Improper beaming. (Should be in groups of two eighth notes or all notes beamed together.)
      2. Stem direction should be down above the third line of the staff.
   c. Improper beaming. (First eighth note should not be beamed with the others.)
   d. Half rest should not be used in this location. Should be two quarter rests.
   e. 1. Notes in first chord not in proper relationship. (d should be to the left of the stem and e to the right.)
      2. Crescendo should be below the staff.
      3. Chord on the second beat of the measure should be notated as a quarter tied to an eighth to show the third beat of the measure.
      4. Stem direction should be up on the chord on beat four.
   f. Not enough beats in this measure.
   g. The dotted half rest should not be used here. (Should be quarter rest followed by half rest to show the third beat of the measure.)
4. Notes in parentheses are enharmonic equivalents.

   a. d (e♭♭)   b. g (f𝄪)   c. c (b♯)

   d. g (a♭♭)   e. f (e♯)   f. a (b♭♭)

Test Yourself 2 (page 15)

1. a. d harmonic minor   b. E major

   c. f♮ minor   d. g melodic minor (ascending)

2. Names in parentheses are the minor scales.

   a. D (b)   b. E♭ (c)   c. D♭ (b♭)   d. E (c♯)

3. a. C and F   b. D and A   c. B♭ and E♭   d. G and D   e. G♭ and C♭

4. a. D major

   b. A♭ major

   c. B ascending melodic minor

   d. C♯ harmonic minor

5. a. Phrygian mode

   b. Dorian mode

   c. Mixolydian mode

   d. Lydian mode

   e. Phrygian mode

Test Yourself 3 (page 26)

1. P1, m3, M3, P5, m6, M6, P8.
2. a. M3   b. M7   c. P4   d. m6   e. m2   f. A4
3. a. m6   b. m2   c. P5   d. M3   e. M7   f. d5
4. a. P1   b. M2   c. m3   d. M3   e. M6   f. m7
   g. m6   h. m10 (m3)   i. m6   j. m3   k. P4   l. m7
   m. m3   n. M2   o. m6   p. M3
5. a. d-sharp   b. c-double sharp   c. a   d. f   e. b-flat   f. d-sharp
6. a. c-sharp   b. a-flat   c. b-double flat   d. c-sharp   e. d-double sharp
   f. a-double flat

Test Yourself 4 (page 31)

1. a. major   b. minor   c. augmented   d. diminished   e. minor   f. major
2. a. A   b. B_{MI} c. $A\flat+$ d. D°   e. G_{MI} f. $D\flat$
3.
a.	tonic	I^6
b.	subdominant	IV
c.	leading tone	$vii°^6$
d.	tonic	I
e.	dominant	V
f.	tonic	I
g.	tonic	I^6_4
h.	dominant	V
i.	tonic	I

4. a. V   b. VI   c. IV   d. III   e. I   f. VII
5. a. vi   b. iv   c. ii   d. v   e. iii   f. i

Test Yourself 5 (page 39)

1. Deceptive
2. Perfect Authentic
3. Plagal
4. Deceptive
5. Half
6. Half
7. Half
8. Half
9. Imperfect Authentic
10. Plagal
11. Perfect Authentic
12. Deceptive
13. Half
14. Plagal
15. Perfect Authentic
16. Deceptive
17. Plagal
18. Half
19. Half
20. Imperfect Authentic
21. Plagal
22. Perfect Authentic
23. Deceptive
24. Imperfect Authentic
25. a. Plagal   b. Deceptive   c. Half   d. Perfect Authentic
    e. Imperfect Authentic
26. a. Accented passing tone   b. 4–3 Suspension   c. Anticipation
    d. 4–3 Suspension   e. Unaccented passing tone   f. Appoggiatura
    g. 7–6 Suspension

Test Yourself 6 (page 59)

Term		Can Be Found In	
		Line(s)	*Number(s)*
1. Internal extension of a phrase (example)		A	5-8 and 9-12
2. Parallel period		A-B	1-24 and 1 24
3. A sequence of two segments of one-half measure each		A-B	13-16, 13-16
4. A retardation		B	21-23
5. An appoggiatura		A, B, C	15
6. A 4–3 suspension		A, B	20-23, 20-23 (inner voice)
7. A sequence of two segments of one full measure each		E	1-8
8. An authentic cadence on F major		B	19-23
9. A half cadence in C major		C	21-23
10. Exact melodic repetition		A and B	1-17 and 1-17
11. A 7–6 suspension		A, B, D	4-5, 8-9; 4-5, 8-9; 10-11
12. A lower neighboring tone		C	17
13. An accented passing tone		C-E	11,20,10
14. A second-inversion triad		B, C, D, E	19, 21, 3, 11, 17
15. An imperfect authentic cadence in C major		E	12-16
16. A phrase member		D, E	1-8, 9-16, 1-8, 9-16
17. A phrase extension near the beginning		A, B	5-8, 5-8
18. A set of contrasting phrases (period)		C-D	C1-23, C23 with D1-20

19. four
20. two
21. The first one is a contrasting period, and the second one is a parallel period.

22. German Folk Song.

Test Yourself 7 (page 64)

1. monophonic texture   __d__
   polyphonic texture   __c__
   homophonic texture   __b__
   homorhythmic texture   __a__
2. primary melody (PM)   __1, 3, 6, 7__
   secondary melody (SM)   __5__
   parallel supporting melody (PSM)   __2__
   static support _____
   harmonic support (HS) _____
   rhythmic support (RS) _____
   harmonic rhythmic support (HRS)   __4__
3. The thinnest texture is example   __d__
4. The thickest texture is example   __a__

5. Beethoven: Sonata, op. 13: III (Allegro), m. 1–8.

6. The right hand part in the preceding example is __PM__ (textural element). The left hand part is __HRS__ (textural element). The excerpt is an example of homophonic texture (texture type).

Test Yourself 8 (page 72)

a.

1	Counterpoint below a *cantus firmus* must begin with an octave or unison, not a fifth.
1–8	Too many repeated notes.
4–6	Climax tone repeated.
6–7	Parallel fifths.
8–10	G-natural too close to G-sharp.
9–10	Augmented second, not an allowable interval.

b.

3–6	Too much parallel motion.
8–9	Similar (hidden) fifths.
10–11	Not a correct ending—should end with an octave or unison.

Four leaps (4–5, 7–8, 8–9, 9–10).

Melodic contour deficient—no ascent to climax tone, followed by descent.

c.

2–5	Interval between *c.f.* and cpt. greater than a 10th.
9	Interval between *c.f.* and cpt. greater than a 10th.
10–13	Too much parallel motion.

Four leaps (1–2, 2–3, 5–6, 9–10).

d.

4	Unison not allowed in the middle of a counterpoint.
4–5	Octaves by contrary motion.
7–8	Similar (hidden) octaves.
8–12	Too much parallel motion.

Repeated melodic segment (1–4, 9–12).

Four leaps (4–5, 7–8, 8–9, 12–13).

Range of counterpoint covers a minor seventh—not a good range.

Test Yourself 9 (page 81)

1. Errors are listed below:

1–2	Similar (hidden) octaves—soprano and bass.
3	Diminished triad in root position—should only be used in first inversion.
5–6	Parallel octaves and fifths.
9	No third factor.
12	No third factor.
12–13	Parallel octaves—tenor and soprano.
13	Doubled leading tone.

2.

Keep the common tone

a.

CM: I   IV

Two common tones

b.

vi   IV

Contrary motion in the upper parts

c.

IV   V

Double bass on dim. triad

d.

6

I   vii°⁶

Keep the common tone

e.

CM: ii   V

f.

or

I⁶   IV

Double bass on second inversion

g.

6
4

IV   I⁶₄

Don't double the leading tone

h.

or

6

V   V⁶

Test Yourself 10 (page 95)

1. a. 1, 5, 7, 8, 10, 12, 14, 15, 16
   b. (none)
   c. 2, 9
   d. 3, 4, 6, 11, 13
2. Circle progressions are more common than other progressions.
3. Circles indicate chord choices. Other answers are possible.

O Ewigkeit, du Donnerwort (Oh Eternity, Thou Word of Thunder)

(15 circle progressions, 1 weaker circle progression)

4. Bach's setting of the chorale is on page 179.

Test Yourself 11 (page 106)

1. a. G, bass, B
   b. B, alto, D
   c. Db, alto, F
   d. Bb, alto, Db
   e. A, soprano, C
   f. Eb, tenor, G
2. 3, 6, 9, and 11
3. 6
4. a. PT   b. 4–3 SUS   c. PT   d. APP   e. PT   f. PT   g. PT
5. a. deceptive   b. half   c. imperfect authentic

Test Yourself 12 (page 118)

1. a. 1, 7, 8, 10, 13, 14, 20
   b. 3, 4, 17, 18
   c. 6, 12
   d. 9, 15, 16
   e. 2, 11
   f. 5, 19
2. a. Parallel 5ths (alto and tenor)   b. 7th of the chord does not resolve downward by step
   c. Parallel 5ths (tenor and bass)

Test Yourself 13 (page 128)

1. a. No error
   b. Parallel 5ths (soprano and tenor)
   c. A2nd (alto)
   d. No error
   e. A2nd (alto), 7th of the chord does not resolve downward by step.
   f. 7th of the chord does not resolve downward by step.
   g. No error
   h. 7th of the chord does not resolve downward by step.
   i. No error

2. a. ii^7 V
   b. IV^7 VII
   c. VI^7 ii
   d. iii^7 vi
   e. ii^{ø7} V
   f. I^7 IV

Test Yourself 14 (page 138)

1. b. DM: I   ii   IV   vi
       GM: IV   vi   I   iii
   c. f♯m: i   ii°   III iv   v   VI   VII
       AM: vi   vii° I   ii   iii IV   V
   d. em: i   III   iv   VI
       CM: iii   V   vi   I
   e. fm: i   III   iv   VI
       D♭M: iii   V   vi   I
   f. BM: I   iii   V   vi
       d♯m: VI   i   III iv
   g. g♯m: i   ii°   iv   VI
       BM: vi   vii° ii   IV
   h. gm: I
       dm: iv
   i. EM: I   ii   IV   vi
       f♯m: VII   i   III v

Test Yourself 15 (page 154)

1.

a.

b.

c.

V^6_5/V in the key of A♭ major-minor

V^6_5/ii in the key of D♭ major

V^6_5/iv in the key of b♭ minor

V^6_5/vi in the key of G♭ major

V^6_5/iii in the key of C♭ major

V^6/ii in the key of C major

V^6/VI in the key of f♯ minor

V^6/iii in the key of B♭ major

V^6/V in the key of G major-minor

V^6/IV in the key of A major

$vii°^7/iv$ in the key of d minor

$vii°^7/iii$ in the key of E♭ major

$vii°^7/V$ in the key of C major-minor

$vii°^7/ii$ in the key of F major

$vii°^7/VI$ in the key of b minor

2.

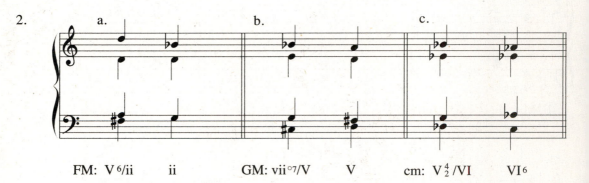

FM: V^6/ii ii   GM: $vii°^7/V$ V   cm: V^4_2/VI VI^6

E♭M: $vii°^7/iii$ iii   CM: $vii°^6/V$ V   b♭m: V^6_5/VI VI   f♯m: V/VII   VII
                                                                                           (natural)

cm: $vii°^7/iv$ iv   D♭M: $vii°^6_5/ii$ ii^6 am: $vii°^4_2/V$ V^6_4 AM: $vii°^7/vi$ vi

Test Yourself 16 (page 158)

1. The first section (measures 1–8) is open since it ends with a half cadence (away from the tonic chord). The second section (measures 9–18) is closed since it ends on the tonic.
2. The first section (measures 1–8) is open since it ends in the relative major (away from the *original* tonic chord). The second section (measures 9–34) is closed since it ends on the *original* tonic.
3. A *phrase* is a substantial musical thought usually ending with both a harmonic and melodic cadence. Two or more adjacent phrases may combine to form a *period*. An important characteristic of period construction is a relatively weaker cadence at the end of the first phrase (or phrases), and a strong cadence at the end of the final phrase. A *section* is a major division of a part form. Each section is a complete musical statement. By the definitions above, a *phrase* can never be a *period*, since a period must consist of two or more phrases. However, a *section* may (and often does) consist of a single *period*, so a period can be a section.

Test Yourself 17 (page 160)

1. The first section (measures 1–16) is closed, since it ends on the tonic chord (C major).
2. The second section (measures 17–32) is open, since it ends away from the original tonic chord (A♭ major).
3. The B section acts as a contrasting section to the A section. It is often in a different key and has different melodic and rhythmic material. After the B section, the return to the A section is more pleasing, since it sounds "new" again.
4. In the *rounded binary form* the repetition of the first section (sometimes in part) occurs *within* the second section of the piece. It is not a separate section in itself. The rounded binary form retains its essential division into two parts.
5. The auxiliary members mentioned in the text are: introduction, transition, and coda.

Anthology

Bach: *Christus, der ist mein Leben* (Christ Is My Life), BWV 281.

Bach: *Gottes Sohn ist kommen* (The Son of God Has Come), BWV 318.

Bach: *Jesu, du mien liebstes Leben* (Jesus, Thou My Dearest Life), BWV 356.

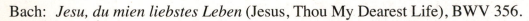

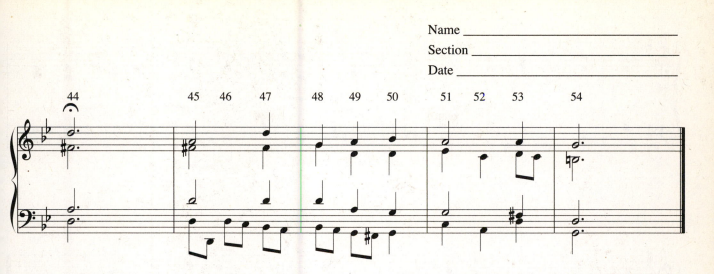

Bach: *O Ewigkeit, du Donnerwort* (Oh Eternity, Thou Word of Thunder), BWV 20, (incomplete).

Bach: *O Herre Gott, dien göttlich Wort* (Oh Lord Our God, Thy Holy Word), BWV 184.

Bach: Sarabande from French Suite no. 1, BWV 812, in D Minor.

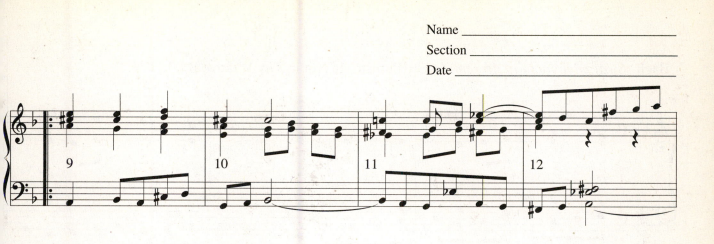

Bach: *Straf mich nicht in deinem Zorn*   (Punish Me Not in Thy Wrath), BWV 115.

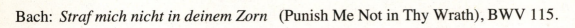

Bach: *Werde munter, mein Gemüte* (Sink Not Yet, My Soul to Slumber), BWV 55.

B♭M: I   IV⁶ ___ vi⁷ ___ ___ ___ ___ ___ iii⁷ ___ ii⁶₅

* Melodic minor

___ ___ ___ ii°⁶₅ ___ ___ ___ ___ ___ ___ ___ ii°⁶₅ ___ ___ ___

___ ___ ___ vi⁷ ___ ___ ___ ___ ___ ___ ___ ii⁶₅ ___ ___ ___

Bartók: Bagatelle, op. 6, no. 5, m. 30–47.

poco **sf**

Bartók: Rumanian Folk Song

Andante (♩ = 104)

harsany hangon

Beethoven: Sonata in C Minor *(Pathétique)*, op. 13, I (Grave), m. 1–11.

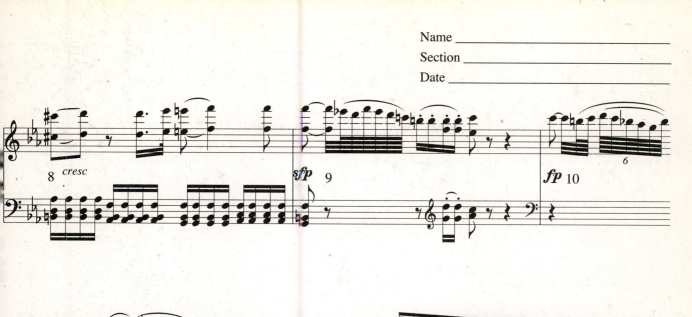

attacca subito il Allegro

Beethoven: Sonata in E-flat Major, op. 31, no. 3, III (Menuetto).

TRIO

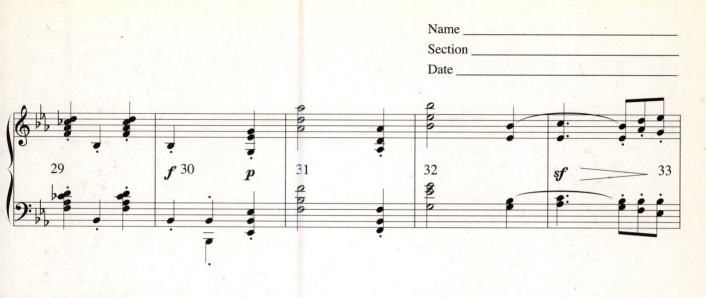

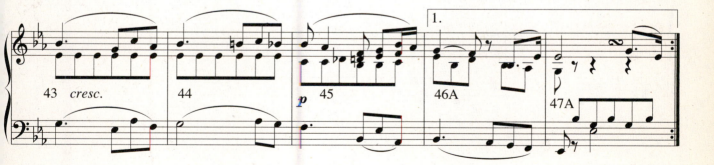

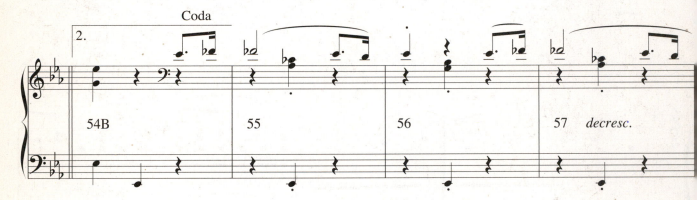

Beethoven: String Quartet in C Minor, op. 18, no. 4, IV (Allegro), m. 1–40.

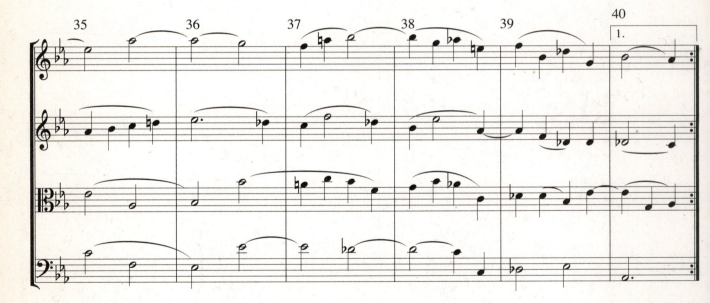

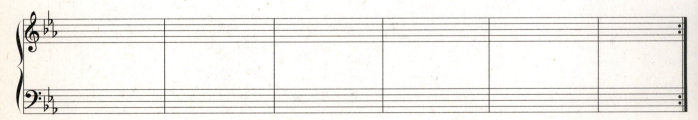

Beethoven: *Thema* from *Sechs Variationen* in D Major (for piano), op. 76.

Brahms: *Sehnsucht* (Longing) from Songs and Romances, op. 14, no. 8.

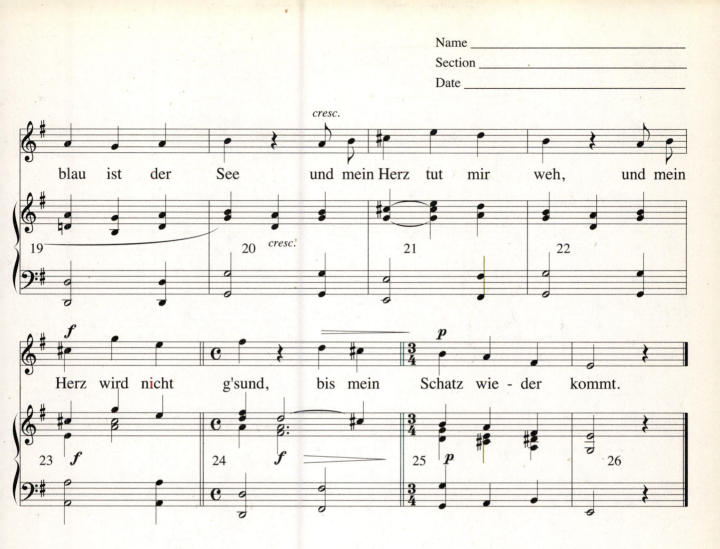

blau ist der See und mein Herz tut mir weh, und mein

Herz wird nicht g'sund, bis mein Schatz wie - der kommt.

Corelli: Corrente.

Vivace

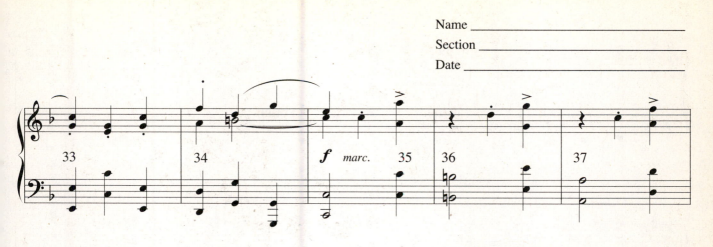

Corelli: Largo.

Couperin: *Rigaudon* from *Pièces de clavecin* (Pieces for the Harpsichord), Second Order.

Interval between highest and lowest voice:

P8		m3	m3	P5	P8												
1		2	3	4	5	6	7	8	9	10	11	12	13	14	15	16	17

Anthology

Farnaby: The New Sa-Hoo (written circa 1595) from the Fitzwilliam Virginal Book.

* Executed as two eighth notes of the same pitch.

Grieg: *Volkweise* (Folk Song) from Lyric Pieces, op. 38, no. 2.

Handel: Gigue from Harpsichord Suite no. 7 in B-flat Major.

Handel: "Hallelujah!" from *Messiah* (choral parts only).

Kings, and Lord of Lords, and He shall reign for - ev - er and ev -

and He shall reign for - ev - er and ev - er and ev -

King of Kings, and Lord of Lords,

er, for - ev - er and ev - er for - ev - er and ev - er, Hal - le - lu - jah, Hal - le -

er,

lu - jah, Hal - le - lu - jah, Hal - le - lu - jah, Hal - le - lu - jah!

Handel: Sarabande from Harpsichord Suite no. 4 in E Minor.

Handel: Sarabande from Harpsichord Suite no. 5 in E Minor.

Haydn: Sonata in A Major, Hob XVI:12, II (Menuet).

*Ignore the B-flat in answering question 5.

Menuet da Capo

Haydn: Sonata in E Major, Hob. XVI:13, II (Menuet), m.1–24.

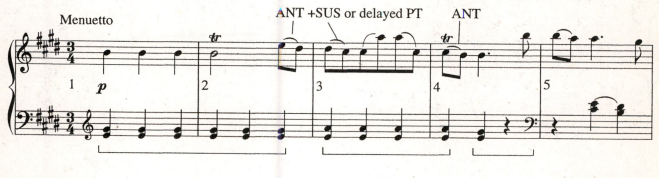

EM: I   IV$_4^6$ I

V^7 I

vii°/V

*Retardation

*Retardation = Suspension which resolves upward.

Haydn: Sonata in E Minor, Hob. XVI:34, III (Molto Vivace), m. 1-18.

Molto Vivace

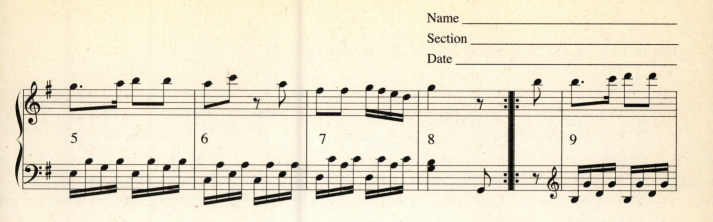

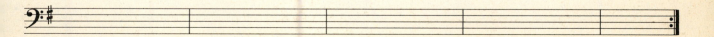

Haydn: Sonata in C Major, Hob. XVI:35, III (Finale), m. 1–25.

* Consider some possible contrapuntal chords here.

Kuhlau: Sonatina in F Major, op. 55, no. 4, II (Andante con espressione).

Andante con espressione

Kuhlau: Sonatina in G Major, op. 88, no. 2, II (Andante Cantabile).

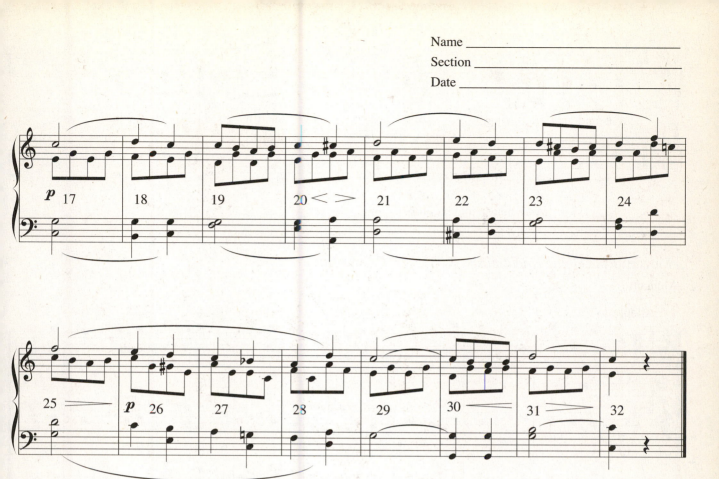

Lowell Mason: "Joy to the World!" (attributed to Handel).

Joy to the world! the Lord is come: Let earth re - ceive her King; Let

ev - ery heart pre - pare Him room, and heav-n and na - ture sing, and

And heav'n and na - ture

heav-n and na - ture sing, And heav'n and heav'n and na - ture sing.

And heav'n and na - ture sing,

Mozart: *Eine kleine Nachtmusik,* K. 525, III (Menuetto).

Menuetto

Allegretto

Fine

Menuetto da capo

Mozart: Sonata in A Minor, K. 310, III (Presto), m. 183–252.

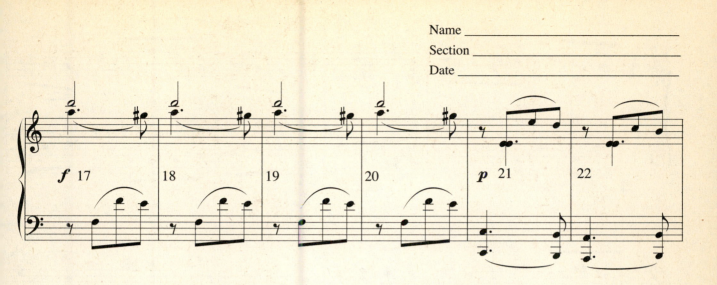

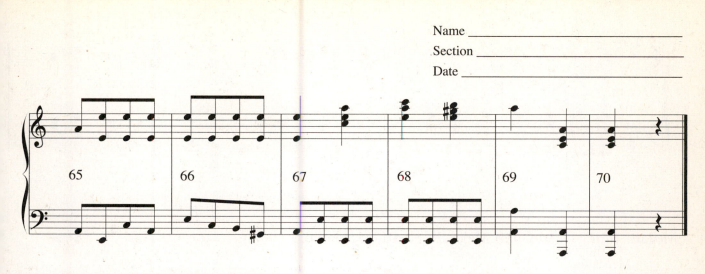

Mozart: Sonata in A Major, K. 331, I (Andante grazioso).

Mozart: String Quartet in G Major, K. 80, III (Menuetto).

Trio

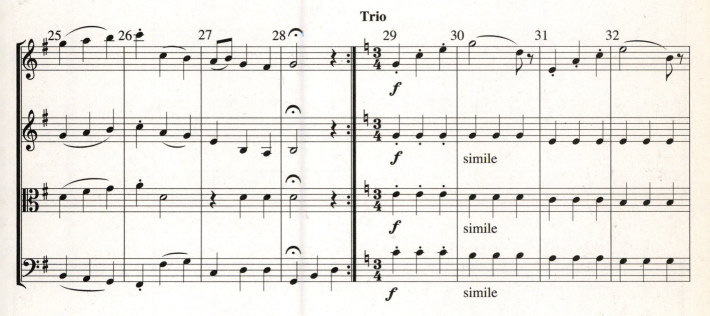

Menuetto da capo

Name _____

Section _____

Date _____

Nicolai: *Wachet auf, ruft uns die Stimme* (Awake! Cries to Us the Voice).

CM:

GM: CM:

CM: CM:

am: CM: CM:

Schubert: German Dance, D. 975.

Schumann: *Davidsbündlertänze*, op. 6, no. 8.

Frisch   ♩ = 100

Schumann: *Erinnerung* (Remembrance) from Album for the Young, op. 68, no. 28.

Nicht schnell une sehr gesangvoll zu spielen (MM ♩ = 66)
Moderato e cantabile assai

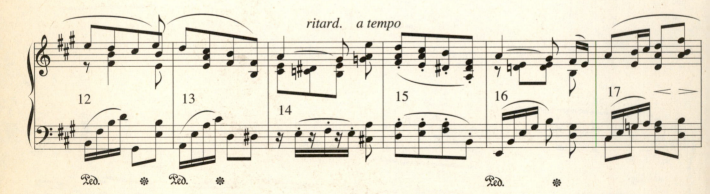

Schumann: *Freu dich sehr, o meine Seele* (Rejoice, O my Soul) from Album for the Young, op. 68, no. 4.

GM: DM: GM:

DM: GM:

Schumann: *Kleine Romanze* (Little Romance) from Album for the Young, op. 68, no. 19.

Nicht Schnell (MM ♩=130)
Non presto

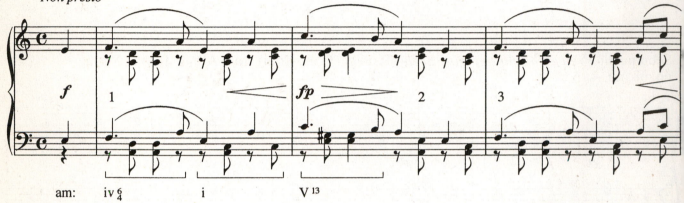

ii$^{\sharp}$ $^6_5$

ii$^{\sharp}$ $^6_5$

Schumann: *Wilder Reiter* (Wild Rider) from Album for the Young, op. 68, no. 8.

Anthology